Sex for Christians

Sex for Christians

The Limits and Liberties of Sexual Living

Revised Edition

Lewis B. Smedes

WILLIAM B. EERDMANS PUBLISHING COMPANY
GRAND RAPIDS, MICHIGAN

Copyright © 1976, 1994 by Wm. B. Eerdmans Publishing Co.
255 Jefferson Ave. S.E., Grand Rapids, Michigan 49503

Printed in the United States of America

09 08 07 06 05 04 03   12 11 10 9 8 7 6

Library of Congress Cataloging-in-Publication Data

Smedes, Lewis B.
Sex for Christians: the limits and liberties of sexual living /
Lewis B. Smedes. — Rev. ed.
p.   cm.
ISBN 0-8028-0743-7
1. Sexual ethics. 2. Sex — Religious aspects — Christianity. 3. Sex in marriage.
4. Christian ethics. I. Title.
HQ32.S55 1994
261.8'344 — dc20   94-12001
CIP

In memory of
my dear friend
Calvin Bulthuis

Contents

Foreword

This book is for people who are trying to get their sexual lives and their Christian lives together. So it is for almost every Christian person I know. All of us have been touched by the sexual revolution in one way or another. On one hand, it has sometimes felt like a tidal wave that could drown an entire generation; on the other, it has stimulated many of us to seek more sexual fulfillment in our own lives. We have drawn back from what looks like sexual chaos and moral turbulence, but we have been drawn toward a larger measure of sexual happiness. We are not always sure whether we are being seduced into a sexual wilderness or beckoned toward sexual freedom. We are being tugged in both directions. The problem is that the difference is often hard to recognize. So I wrote this book as a guide for people who are groping their way into a liberated *and* Christian experience of sexuality.

Any book on sexual morality is a risk. The subject agitates a sensitive impulse of a most delicate dimension of our being. Our sexual nerves weave through the whole fabric of our lives, carrying conflicting messages back and forth from our genitals to our souls. They carry the freight of childhood fears; they throb to the tempo of our adult erotic needs. And they vibrate confusingly with duty and desire, fear and need, memory and fantasy. So when we talk candidly about sexual morality, few of us can keep our cool. And we feel more uneasy the closer we get to specifics like masturbation, petting, premature ejaculation, and oral copulation. We rightly suspect that when sexual morals change, something basic to human life is going to be affected. And we are not always sure whether the change is likely to be for good or evil. In the face of this, a safe way to write about sex for Christian people is to deal profoundly with generalities and to sprinkle them with alarms about the degeneracy of our times. I have not taken this route. I have tried to suggest a morality that, within a biblical perspective, is as liberating as it is limiting. And for that, a little risk is worth taking.

Books on sexual morals are risky for another reason. The subject itself is very elusive: it has too many shapes and colors for anyone to capture all of it in one piece. It ranges from the deep dynamics of our humanness to concrete questions like whether Christians ought to look at pornography. It moves from the primordial issues of maleness and femaleness to painful encounters with frigid wives and impotent husbands. It leaps the fences of ordinary argument into dark corners of subconscious fears. No two people look at their own sexual problems and potentials with the same combination of reason and feeling. Further, it is very hard to pinpoint the special moral dimension of sexual behavior: it is hard to keep clear the difference between the feelings of sexual frustration and the feelings of moral guilt, between feeling personal distaste and making objective moral judgments, and between feeling good and being right. How can we locate that special aspect of sexual life that we call *moral?* To try is to take a risk. But it cuts so close to people's real lives that the risk is worth taking.

One way to get to the moral heart of sexual relationships is to focus only on the personal quality expressed in them. A good deal of Christian morality is following this line these days. The moral question on this route is not whether a particular act is right or wrong; it is only whether the personal equation turns out to be loving and creative. I have argued that, from the Christian perspective, some sexual actions carry moral qualities in themselves apart from whether the persons involved mean well by each other. However, I also believe that many forms of sexual behavior are good or bad depending wholly on whether they convey a sharing of love and pleasure. The Christian person has to learn where to make the distinction.

I hope it will be clear that I have wanted to let compassion be the cutting edge of morality. I have written in compassion for people who are too heavy-laden with moral rules to be sexually free; I have written in compassion for people who walk the border between the pain of sexual need and the demands of moral law; and I have written in compassion for people who have too easily abandoned moral law in their pursuit of sexual happiness. I hope this book may help liberate some, and that it may help others to find freedom within moral boundaries. In any case, I will be pleased if it stimulates anyone to try to think about his own sexual experience within a Christian framework.

The book is divided into three sections. The first is about human sexuality — its created goodness, its sinful distortions, and its redeemed potential. Here we stride across the broad ranges of what we *are* as human sexual beings. The second and third sections are about sexual behavior — the things we *do*. Some readers may want to move directly to the second section and begin with specific problems concerning rights and wrongs in things we do. Afterward, they may be inclined to go back to the beginning for a deeper look at sexuality in general and their own in particular.

My arguments stand pretty much on their own. I decided rather early not to support them by copious quotation. Descriptive material comes from my own study, observation, and counseling. As for my moral arguments, I have tried to let the biblical message control my reasoning. So even when I am not quoting biblical texts I hope it will be clear that I want the gospel to play a steady stream of light on our sexual scene. What I am after is a Christian perspective for a truly human sexual life.

On a less lofty matter, I should say something about my use of pronouns. Writing about sexual relations involves the use of many personal pronouns that might properly be either masculine or feminine. I have often resorted to the device of "he/she" or "him/her." But where I have slipped into a mere "he" or "him," I will leave it to the reader's imagination to substitute a "she" or "her" — or vice versa — whenever it seems right. If the antecedent is impersonal or indefinite, I have stuck to the traditional "he" — with no prejudice intended.

Finally, I must say a word of thanks to Yvonne Geiger, who so expertly and cheerfully typed the bulk of the manuscript for this book. I owe thanks to several people who read it in manuscript and who made many useful suggestions and criticisms, but especially to Clifford Penner, who criticized it from the viewpoint of the clinical psychologist; to my students Karen Kiser and Georgianne Rodiger, who, besides correcting some male prejudices, made valuable stylistic suggestions; and, finally, to my wife Doris, without whom — for many reasons — the book would probably not have been written at all.

PART ONE

SEX AND
CHRISTIAN PEOPLE

CHAPTER ONE

How Do You Feel about It?

The toughest problem Christians have with sex is how to feel about their own sexuality. On this subject many of us are confused, confounded, and inconsistent. We may be sure that we know what is right or wrong about things people do with sex, especially things other people do. But few of us really are sure within ourselves about how we actually feel and how we ought to feel about the sexuality that is woven into the texture of our very beings. The most sex-frightened prude may secretly enjoy the sexual urges that pulsate within him/her. The most liberated person of our supposedly taboo-free age has residual tinges of shame about his/her sexuality. The one is ashamed of the urges he cannot help nourishing inside himself; the other is embarrassed by the shame he cannot get rid of. Few of us totally deny our sexuality. But we cannot find the way into a happy celebration of it either. We carry a complex mixture of feelings.

The average Christian has an especially hard time integrating his sexuality with his faith. He is dedicated to a Lord whose earthly life was celibate and whose messengers were not interested in reporting his attitudes toward sex. He is summoned to follow the Lord into purity and holiness, neither of which is usually allowed

3

to include an enthusiastic summons to sexual fulfillment. He is informed and guided by Scripture, whose word on sexuality is not always specific and clear. He senses that he ought not feel right about anything that his Lord feels less than enthusiastic about. Does God like sex? Would Jesus be pleased with our restless urges, our fantasies, our irrational itching for sexual experience? Can we integrate sexuality with Christian sanctification? Can a Christian person think about the mystery of his own sexuality and rejoice and be glad in it?

Those who are sensitive to the tensions within life have always been saddled with the job of reconciling two competing currents within human experience. One current is vital, dynamic, moving, and restless: it is the spontaneous, palpable vitality of nature. Here we experience the irrational, sometimes upheaving, movement of nature toward birth and growth. On this side of life humanness throbs with needs for explosive release of energy, impulsiveness, and ecstasy. The other current is thoughtful, orderly, controlled, and rational. In it we experience the need for discipline, the desire to keep things in order and to mold raw life into shapes and forms designed by our minds. Here we want to keep vitality under control; here we discipline our impulses; here we fence in the restless drives that rise from the energy cells of life.

The reason Christians have a special problem is that the tensions we feel in our sexuality often seem to fit Paul's label "the lusts of the flesh." If our lives are guided by the Spirit, we will not fulfill "the cravings of our lower nature" (Gal. 5:16). How, then, can we bring our sexuality into Christian discipleship except as that murky side of us which ought to be put down by the Spirit? Christian commitment, it seems to many, places us on the side of God against our sexual drives. We may say that sexuality is good in itself, but only needs control. But the fact that it needs so much control easily creates the feeling that our sexuality is a threat to our Christian lives, a threat percolating up from the dark abyss of our old nature.

4

Some Christians feel that their sexuality is nature's strongest competitor for their loyalty to Christ: "You cannot love both God and sex." While they may not make it part of their creed, their feelings tell them that sexuality is not a sweet gift of creation but a bitter fruit of the fall. They are supported in this by a long antisexual tradition within Christianity. Augustine, to whom we otherwise owe more than most of us even imagine, interpreted the Christians' calling to struggle against evil as a calling to struggle against their sexuality. Intense desires for sexual fulfillment and intense pleasure from sexual action were for him marks of fallen man. Augustine could not imagine an innocent person in Paradise turned on sexually: a sinless Adam could never have been sexually aroused by a pure Eve; Adam and Eve could not have walked with God in the day and made spontaneous love at night. If we do this now it is only because we have not brought our bodies under the rule of Christ. The less one is driven toward sex and the less pleasure he receives from sexual expression, the more sure he can be of his own sanctification. The Lord, in his grace, tolerates our inconsistency; but we must know that he calls us to better, sexless things. This was how Augustine felt about sexuality. Some Christians still carry Augustine's feelings in their hearts; they can only hope that God tolerates their sexuality until their liberation from it in heaven.

Other Christians, who have perhaps grown up during the sexual revolution, have thrown off their guilt feelings about sexuality. But they have still not found a way to mesh their good feelings about sexuality into their commitment to Christ. They are persuaded that Christ is somehow a friend of sexuality, but they suspect that the church is not. They live in a kind of duality: on the one hand they feel right about affirming their sexuality, and on the other they accept a view of Christian faith in which sex, while not condemned, has no positive place. They accept restrictions on their sexual behavior but do not know how to thank God for their sexuality even within the rules of morality.

5

They feel they have a right to enjoy their sexuality, but they don't know how it fits into their Christian life. And they resent the church's inability to help them celebrate their sexuality while respecting its limits and liberties.

The next three chapters ask how our sexuality fits into the same picture with God. This is really a way of asking how we are invited by God to feel about our sexuality within and not alongside our Christian faith. Here we will be laying the groundwork of sexual morality.

Sexual morality, first of all then, has to do with how we ought to feel about ourselves as sexual beings. It has to do with our attitudes toward all the desires and pleasures, the needs and their satisfactions, that are bound up with our sexuality. A good sexual life has to do with more than how people act and by what rules they regulate their behavior. Many people who obey the traditional rules of Christian morality live a miserable sexual existence. Equally true is the fact that many liberated people who fly free and easy over all the traditional sexual moral codes are left barren and lonely as sexual persons. Coming to terms with how Christians are invited by their faith to feel about their sexuality ought to open the door to a kind of peace of conscience and personal enjoyment that is not alien to but an essential part of their Christian discipleship. However, plowing through to a Christian celebration of sexuality is not all that easy; nor is the way through the Bible and tradition all that clear.

At this point, I ought to say something more about what I mean by sexuality. Sexuality refers to what we are, not only what we do. What we are cuts across what we do, to be sure; some of us never really come to terms with what we are until we begin doing. Few of us are ever sure of how we feel about what we are until after we do something that reveals something new about ourselves. An adolescent may not really come to terms with his sexual feelings in any deep sense until he masturbates or engages in petting. Some people do not really confront their feelings about sexuality until they discover the freedom to talk about it late in life. Some people never face up to their feelings. But even though we often are plugged into our feelings only after we act, our feelings about what we *are* can be distinguished from our sense of right and wrong concerning what we *do*.

Our sexuality penetrates several dimensions of our lives. The first level of sexuality is physical — partly neurological, partly a matter of hormones, and partly a matter of touch, taste, sight, and smell. What do we experience when we experience sexuality on this level? We feel caught up in the pulsating vitality of body-life: we are part of the rising and falling of sheer physical dynamics and tension. We feel a tension that is not easily relaxed, an urge that is not easily quenched, a desire that is not easily satisfied, a chafing within that is not easily soothed. And all this is focused — sometimes only vaguely — on our genitals or breasts. In the process we may fantasize about a particular person, but the aiming of our desire at that person is secondary to the vague and undirected desire. We do not *choose* to be involved in this tension; it comes with us as part of our sexuality, part of our selves. In this level of our being, we seem far removed from the spiritual life. Here we deal with spontaneous, unchosen urges that can easily seem like a threat to everything we value as Christian — prayer, devotion, purity, beauty, and the love of God. The question is whether it *must* be felt as a threat to the life of the soul.

Our sexuality always leads us beyond the physical stage to a far more personal need: we are driven inexorably into a desire for personal, intimate involvement with another person. The glandular urge, it turns out, is the undercurrent of a need for sharing ourselves with another person. Sexuality throbs within us as movement toward relationship, intimacy, companionship. The desire is more than a wish for somebody's fingers to play with our bodies, though it is that also; it is an exciting desire, sometimes a melancholy longing, to give ourselves in trust to another. We want to expose our whole selves to another and to be trusted with another person's self-exposure to us; we want to stretch out and reach into another person so that the other can add himself to what we are; we want to probe into the mystery of another person's being. It is also a feeling that we cannot be complete until we give ourselves to another person. This is to say that our biological sexuality is lifted into personal *eros*.

This brings us to still another level of our sexuality: the need for self-knowledge. We need to explore the mystery of another person in order to get inside the mystery of ourselves. The two — the biological and the interpersonal — must come together as our passage into self-knowledge. Our sexuality whispers a promise that if we could really get close to it, really express it, really satisfy it, we would come into our own as persons. This is why, in some fuzzy sense, everyone associates sexual maturity with growing up. The intuition is that knowing oneself as a person is tied up with knowing another person sexually. Our sexuality, then, is a biologically rooted urge to answer the ancient counsel: "Know thyself."

Is there more? There probably is. There is probably more to our sexuality than meets the eye or is open to our conscious experience. Why have people often associated sex with religion, as though somehow sex were the gateway to God? What distorted vision of reality led those ancient Canaanites to their shrines of prostitution? What was it, on the other hand, that led Paul to see marriage as an illustration of how Christ relates to the church and to see sexual intercourse as a mysterious life-uniting act that so radically altered the partners' individual existence that they became one flesh? Christianity knows that we do not get to God through ecstasy of the flesh. But the ecstasy of sexual fulfillment is not absolutely unlike the ecstasy of religious experience, otherwise it would not have been so often identified with it. Is there more to our sexuality than the share we have in animal nature, more than the urge for personal union, more even than the discovery of our selves? Is there more than meets the eye of the sexologist?

Our sexuality is hard to categorize because it spills over into so many levels of our life. But hard as it is to catch it in a neat verbal net, we know that it is woven into all that we are as personal creatures of this world. The question is how we should value it, how we should feel about it, how we should relate it to our conviction that to love and serve God and our neighbor is the one thing necessary.

We must turn to the Bible. But where shall we turn, and how shall we read? Must we look for texts that will tell us how to feel? We will be hard put to find many; the Bible does not spell out divine theories of sexuality. Nor is it a book with only one response to sexuality: its several writers always write in response to the needs and conditions of their situation. Many Old Testament writers have one eye slanted toward the pagan religions, and their warnings against certain sexual practices are often a warning against a religion that turns worship into a sex orgy. Jesus talks amid legalistic Jews, reminding them that sexual chastity is not bought simply by avoiding illegal acts. Further, he sees marriage as rooted in creation and thus evidently thinks very highly of it. Paul, on the other hand, expecting Christ to return soon, at first sees no great value in marriage, except as a way to cabin and control sexual drives.

If there is one clear endorsement of sexual passion — besides the Song of Solomon — it is Proverbs 5:18-19:

> Rejoice with the wife of thy youth. Let her be as the loving hind and pleasant roe; let her breasts satisfy thee at all times; and be thou ravished always with her love. (KJV)

True, the point of this verse is that a young man should enjoy the embrace of his own wife rather than be "ravished with a strange woman." But the proverb hardly hints that a man should be ashamed of a sexuality that nudges him toward sensual pleasure. On the other end of the spectrum is the vision of Revelation

14, whose spiritual heroes at the throne of the Lord are chaste elders who were not "defiled with women," but who followed the Lamb faithfully (Rev. 14:4). The impulses that push us toward sexual union are not given a celebrative boost here. The rest of the Bible deals with sexuality somewhere between the boundaries of Proverbs 5:18 and Revelation 14:4.

Sexuality is not something that biblical writers are concerned about in any explicit way, nor does one sense that they were hung up with shame about it. One gets the impression from the Old Testament that the glandular urge was simply assumed as part of male life that had to be put under some limits; female sexuality is hardly recognized. In the New Testament, sexual promptings seem to be more of a threat; it seems far more important to avoid fornication than to fulfill sexual need. The erotic desire for sharing the intimate presence of another person is not a large part of the New Testament scene.

Marriage, for instance, is not lauded as a partnership entered for the enrichment of the lives of the partners. It is, for Paul at least, a way of domesticating sexuality so that it will not spill over into the sin of fornication. Marriage is much more than this, of course. Those splendid passages in Ephesians and Colossians about marriage lift it to a plateau where it can be compared to Christ's union with his church. The marriage *status* has enormous meaning for Paul. But a reader would not get the word from him that sexual union is a gateway to personal enrichment and voluptuous delight. One would not easily guess that Paul might advise a frustrated couple to seek therapy in order to get more pleasure from their sexual union.

In contrast, we live in a time when all levels of sexuality are given top billing in life. Romantic love, the personal side of erotic desire, is accepted as the most beautiful promise in life. Erotic relationships are valued for their potential of happiness. If there is one message we have all heard in our time, it is the tantalizing news that sexuality is a good thing. But for many of us the message has not gone below our mind. We may admit it with our minds, but our feelings carry a suspicion that sexuality is an embarrassment to genuinely Christian people. We still feel uneasy, restless, embarrassed by the vital urges within us. But either way — as a promise or a problem — sexuality has become a major concern. It is at or near the top of our priorities. We have been talking about it, viewing it with alarm, disturbed by what we see around us, and stimulated by what we feel within us. But we have not yet — many of us — come to terms with it.

The writers of the Bible did not make sexuality a major theme. They had more urgent matters on their minds: they were responding to the great acts of God for human salvation. They were not divinely inspired to theorize about sex. But it was just because they were bringing the good news for the whole person that they could not help saying something about human sexuality.

How then can we read the Bible as an informing light for our sexual lives? This is a pivotal question. I think, in the first place, that we can let the gospel open up a *perspective* for us on human life as a whole. The message of Christ gives us a point of view, a vista from which to understand and evaluate our total experience as human beings. It informs our attitudes, shapes our values, and points to our goals. It also speaks to us about our origins as body-persons, and about our inevitable tendency to distort life. And it offers the possibility of liberation from the powers of distortion and inhumanity. In short, what we look for first is not a theory of sexuality nor a set of rules for sexual behavior; we look for an understanding of what we are, what we tend to make of ourselves, and what we can be through grace. And then we can fit our sexuality and our sexual behavior into the biblical pattern and the biblical perspective. What we want, then, is not sexual information first of all, but a view and an attitude toward our sexual lives that is informed by the gospel as a whole.

The wrong way would be to look only for biblical texts that

tell us what to do and what not to do in sex. There are rules, to be sure. And any Christian will take them seriously. But what we need to find out is whether there is an insight, a vision, that tells us what the deeper significance of sexuality and sexual behavior is. For instance, we want to know more than the New Testament rules about extramarital sex; we want to know the New Testament insight into the significance of sexual intercourse. Only then can we make sense of the rules. It is a mistake to think of the New Testament as a new revelation of rules for sexual behavior. The New Testament is a message of grace; it is the gospel of freedom in Christ. Through it we come face to face with God's movement toward us so that we can move toward him and toward each other. To locate the real message of the Bible concerning sexuality, we will have to see how our sexuality and our sexual living is embraced within the gospel. If we can manage that, we will be in a position to discern the limits implicit in the liberty — and the liberty within the limits — of our sexual life in Christ.

CHAPTER TWO

Let Us Rejoice and Be Glad in It

How to feel about our sexuality is part of a larger question. For the Christian believer, at any rate, the larger question is how to feel about creation. If our sexuality belongs to creation, our feelings about it can be of a piece with God's feelings about what he made. However, our sexuality is the turbulent fountain of so much tension that it has struck many Christians as the clearest example of creation's distortion by sin. In that view, our sexuality drags us downward, shackling us to its urges, while our soul would rather fly with the Lord into freedom. Augustine said: "For my *soul's* freedom I resolved not to desire, nor to seek, nor to marry a wife." The spontaneous impulses of our sexuality seem to counter the Christian call to self-control: "Away with the thought that there should have been any unregulated excitement [in Paradise] . . ." (Augustine). Ecstatic experience in sex scarcely harmonizes with the mandate to subdue the earth or the Christian's summons to present his body as a reasonable service to God. It is altogether too much like apoplexy, madness, and wild torrents of dark passion. Would it not then be prudent for the Christian to play it safe and at least treat sexuality, as we experience it on this side of Eden, as sinful lust?

13

Keeping the good of creation separate from sin's distortions of creation is no easy job. Polluted streams, contaminated air, ruined forests, and deadly cancers are easy to spot and label as distortions of creation. Seduction and rape, unbridled sensuality, sadism and masochism, and personal exploitation are not difficult to identify as sexual distortion. But how do we know whether the early stirrings of sensual pleasure in a child, the genital excitement in an adolescent, the erotic passions of an adult are native to God's good creation or a mangled parody of it? That there is still good in created nature the Bible is certain: "For everything created by God is good, and nothing is to be rejected if it is received with thanksgiving . . ." (I Tim. 4:4). We are to love what God has made, feel good about anything that is human, and hate only what sinful human beings and devils have unmade. The job is to cultivate a good perception for what is of God and what is of sin.

Of course, we could untie the knot by saying that while sexuality as such is good, sexuality as we experience it since the fall is evil. But if we eliminate all the experience of it now, we would have to suppose that good sexuality is empty of intense desires and pleasures as well as its confusing agitations. Thus, no child would have grown up in Paradise discovering that it was pleasant to play with his genitals; no male would have been aroused by an attractive woman; no woman would have felt an unsettling sexual desire stirring inside her. If sexual intercourse did take place only for the sake of having children, it would have occurred with due deliberation, without ecstasy, sweat, or turbulence. Sexual need would merely have felt like the need to urinate. In short, it would have been flat, dull, and endlessly tedious — not the rich and exciting diversity it really is.

There are differences between what is good and what is distorted here in our experience in a sinful world. Sexuality can be distorted, and we had better keep our antennae sensitive to the severe distortions of our day. But this does not mean that all of the lively currents of sexuality we now experience are a distortion of some cold and morbidly dull thing we might imagine sexuality to have been in Paradise.

1. BODY-LIFE

"Then the Lord God formed man of dust from the ground, and breathed into his nostrils the breath of life; and man became a living being" (Gen. 2:7) — we might say a "living body." Here is our deep bond with earth, and at the same time our unique bond with the life-breathing God. I am a spirit-enlivened body: the life is from God, and when he withdraws his breath, the body collapses like a leaky tire (Ps. 104:29; Job 34:14f.). But the body is from the earth, like that of the animals who were brought forth from the ground in the creation story. So our life is body-life; I am a body-person.

Perhaps we can play the theme negatively by noticing what the biblical writer does not say. God is not pictured making a soul and wrapping a body around it. He does not work like a watchmaker, who first crafts the inner works and then inserts it in a case. Nor is the soul set on earth with a body as baggage for its pilgrimage. To belabor the point, the soul does not drive the body around like an angel driving an automobile. The biblical story is not about the creation of a soul that possesses or is encumbered by a body; it is about a body that comes alive to God.

The second creation story (Gen. 2) suggests that a person cannot "know himself" until he comes to terms with his body. We may want to think of ourselves as spiritual and deal with who and what we are only on a spiritual level; but our bodies keep demanding more respect. Further, as the Genesis writer goes on to tell us, we cannot really come to self-knowledge alone. God made a male body-person, and his name was *Ish*. But he was

15

alone. Had *Ish* been asked what it was like to be a male, he would have winced in ignorance: "What is a male?" How could he know what a male was as long as there was no female to make him aware? Yet, there was a kind of semiconscious awareness: it came in the form of restlessness. His heart and body were restless until they found their rest in femaleness. God took care of this. He "caused a deep sleep to fall upon the man, and while he slept took one of his ribs . . . and the rib which the Lord God had taken from the man he made into a woman" (Gen. 2:21-22). This done, God led the female to *Ish* as a father leads a bride to her husband. Adam saw her and intuitively recognized her as the answer for the deep need surging through his body. "This at last is bone of my bones and flesh of my flesh; she shall be called woman *(Ishshah).*" *Ish* and *Ishshah* together — as body-persons. Now the male knew what it was to be a male, for he now saw himself in relation to one who was the same as he, but with the crucial difference.

The male and female know themselves only in relation to each other because they are made for each other. This is the deep origin of the powerful drive of the sexes to come together. It arises from the body-life we share, with a difference. Male and female are driven toward each other until they again become "one flesh" in intimate body-union.

God did not wince when Adam, in seeing Eve, was moved to get close to her. Male and female were created sexual to be sexual together. When Adam and Eve, *Ish* and *Ishshah,* clung together in the soft grass of Eden, wild with erotic passion, and finally fulfilled in their love, we may suppose that God looked on and smiled. It could not have entered God's mind that, when his two creatures were sexually aroused, they were submitting to a demonic lust percolating up from some subhuman abyss to ensnare their virgin souls. Body-persons have a side to them that is wildly irrational, splendidly spontaneous, and beautifully sensuous. This is not a regrettable remnant of the beast in human beings, a fiendish enemy in man's personal cold war within himself. It is a gift that comes along with being body-persons. Some Christians may wish that God had stuck with making angels; but God was delighted to have body-persons.

Lest we suppose that all God wanted with his two partners was for them to sport in sexual play, we should note that his body-persons had other things to do. As *persons* they were summoned to make free decisions of obedience to the God who made them. They were given a job to do in the garden, lest its verdancy turn it into jungle. They would exercise responsibility for the whole of the created world. They were, then, not to be merely sexual creatures; they were to be sexual *persons,* responsive to God's will in their development of his garden; and they were to be in personal communion with each other and with their personal creator.

The spontaneity of the body did not rule out the need for order. Spontaneity is not chaos. Impulse need not mean loss of direction, and human sexuality is not an invitation to wild caprice. But the limits of a riverbed do not restrict the freedom of the river; the limits of purpose and order do not have to dampen the spontaneity of sexuality. We can accept ourselves as body-persons without rejecting ourselves as rational and spiritual persons; and we have more to do as body-persons than look for chances to explode sexually. There is the business of providing food for one another, for arranging life in society, for seeking justice and creating art, for digging out the secrets of nature, and for a million other opportunities to create a culture fitting for body-persons who belong to God. The sexuality of our bodies must mesh with the total task of creating culture together. Sexuality is developed *within* the playground and workspace of human creativity; this is why it has limits as well as liberty.

2. GOD-LIKE SEXUALITY

Genesis 1 is like a liturgical chant; it unrolls in terse, stately cadence, with poetry that rises out of a profound religious faith. Here the creation story is compacted, given without the vivid details of the later story. Man and woman are created together, at once, in God's own likeness. When God made his climactic move, he brought forth in a single breath male and female, both in his image.

> So God created man in his own image, in the image of God he created him: male and female he created them. (Gen. 1:27)

One humanity in two sexually distinct instances — male and female.

When I first heard Karl Barth interpret Genesis as teaching that our sexuality is the God-like in us, I was hard put to take him seriously. But his insight was badly needed, not only to prod us to take the simple statement of the Bible seriously but to get us to re-examine our own feelings about the place of sexuality in our lives. Traditional talk about the image of God in man hardly gives a nod to human sexuality; it assumes that we are God's image in spite of our bodies, not *as* bodies. To zero in on sexuality as the God-like in us seemed to insult God. God is spirit: above all he is sexless. How then can it make sense to suppose that our sexuality is what is Godlike in us?

The ideal human being is not a composite male-female person. A person is either a male or a female, but each is his own full self only in relationship with the other. However, the notion of the male-female person, the androgynous personality, has always been fascinating and has led to some troubling extrapolations. Plato relates the myth of a fall in which the two sexes within a single person separated; the ideal person was divided into a male half-person and a female half-person, both in restless search

18

of their other half. The ideal person was split as a judgment on humans, and it cannot be whole until it is joined as one flesh to the half it lost. Christian tradition has sometimes echoed Plato's myth, with its penchant for interpreting the sexual urges of persons as an aftershock of the fall. The prevailing mood, then, is sadness; we are sexual because we are fallen.

The creation story counters this melancholy feeling by saying that both male and female were not only present at the first moment of man's creation, but that while God created them together, *each* of them was his image. They were created as sexually distinguished individuals; but in their being together *as individuals* they were like God. Adam was an individual person in his own right; but he was in his own right only in communion with Eve. Eve was an individual person in her own right; but she was in her own right only in communion with Adam. Each is whole in himself/herself; but each is whole only in communion with the other. Eve was not Adam's "better half" — nor is any woman a man's half. Male and female are in movement toward each other and yet away from each other, each needing the other to be himself/herself, yet each needing to be an individual in his/her own right.

This brings us to sexuality as God's image. Sexuality is the human drive toward intimate communion. Beyond the glandular impulse, the human sexual urge is always toward another person. We want to experience the other, to trust the other and be trusted by him, to enter the other's life by entering the vital embrace of his/her body. We need finally to experience the other in the rhythm of receiving and giving that can be felt in that passionate encounter called sexual intercourse.

This is why sexuality is the sign and seal of God in our body-life. As bodies we experience the urge first in the vague sense of physical restlessness; as persons we experience it in the desire for a person. Here sexuality emerges as erotic desire. Sexual intercourse — at its best — is an epitome of the responsive life of persons in communion. Only in sexual communion, however, is there the added ingredient that makes it most exciting and dangerous: it is the ingredient of passion and ecstasy, the discarding of restraint and reserve. This is why it has the potential to be the epitome of communion: it involves the greatest amount of personal risk.

Having said that sexuality is a drive that begins in our glands and climaxes in communion, we now add that personal communion is what the image of God is about. Biblical revelation tells us to stop thinking of ourselves as isolated islands of rational God-likeness and think of ourselves instead as coming into real humanity when we live in genuine personal fellowship with others. A single person *is* the image of God; but he is God's image only when he personally relates in love to others.

Now it begins to be clear how our sexuality is, if not the essence as Barth suggests, at least a deep dimension of God-likeness. Our sexuality, on all of its graduated levels, is our deeply human drive toward and our means of discovering human communion at its intimate peak. In the sexual embrace of a man and woman human communion is brought to its living end. We must not drive this ideal to the wall. The Bible describes what is true for most people; but it has plenty of room for exceptions. Too many persons have managed a beautifully whole existence without sexual intercourse to let us suppose that only nonvirgins need apply for full humanity. And too many unwhole and distorted people have jumped into almost any available bed to let us suppose that sexual intercourse is a magic carpet to personhood. A male does not become a person merely by penetrating a female's vagina. Still, we are haunted by the creation phrase: "male and female created he them."

Can a male be a whole person without a personal relationship with a woman? We must remember that male and female can and do relate to each other without touching each other's skin, just as they can be skin-close without relating as persons.

Sexual union is the physical climax of personal communion between a man and a woman. But St. Paul was more than half a person. And although virgins do not experience the climax of sexual-personal existence, they can experience personal wholeness by giving themselves to other persons without physical sex. Through a life of self-giving — which is at the heart of sexual union — they become whole persons. They capture the essence without the usual form.

3. SEXUALITY AND MARRIAGE

Sexuality is what marriage is about. But sexuality is about more than marriage. I do not mean to suggest, of course, that sexual intercourse is *all* that marriage is about. Marriage, as anyone who has been married for a while can testify, is about a lot more than coitus: a home has more rooms than the master bedroom. The business of making marriage work depends on far more than successful bed-partnership. Though marriage is rooted in our total sexual needs and is thus the most important way we have found for expressing ourselves as sexual persons, it is not the only way. A person is a sexual being even if he never marries; a child matures into a sexual person long before he has sexual intercourse. And each, while not married, has to find ways to express his male or female sexuality. Most of us get married as an answer to the call of sexuality: it is a need to commit ourselves to a permanent life of intimacy with another. But not everyone needs to live out his male or female sexuality in a permanent union with one person. Obviously there would be no marriage if there were not sexuality; but there is sexuality without marriage.

Jesus once said something that has made many people suppose that marriage is the only reason for sexuality, that if there were no need for marriage there would be no sexuality. Once in heaven, he said, we will not be married to anyone (Mark 12:25).

Many readers of Jesus' words have thought he meant that there can be no sexuality in heaven; that there can be no males and females relating to each other in the many-colored nuances of their sexual differences. But why should we add so dismal a prospect to Jesus' promise? What the Lord tells us is that in God's kingdom the limits and discipline of the marriage structure will be transcended. On earth most of us have time, energy, and dedication enough for only one other person in committed union; in heaven we will be capable of intimacy unbounded. And the intimacy could be sexual even if it were not physical. We know very little about heaven in general; we know less about its sexual life in particular.

Therefore, I am able to argue only by inference from the conviction that everything right and good in creation will not be destroyed but enhanced in the kingdom of God. To look forward to a sexless eternal life is dismal to anyone who values the varied richness of sexuality as one of the most happy dimensions of God's creation. To read Jesus as offering us the bland prospect of a sexless future is to say that our perfection as human beings requires the rejection of one of the most beautiful parts of our creation. Anyone who believes that God wants us to be fully human may anticipate not less but greater sexuality in the kingdom he promises us. If sexuality is what God gave us to reflect his own life, it would be strange indeed if he de-sexed us as our reward in heaven. And if sexuality is forever, we are doubly assured of its goodness on earth.

I suspect that most people who are shocked at the notion of sexuality in heaven suppose we will all be at least facsimiles of males. St. Augustine, as negative as he was about sexual pleasure, at least argued that women will be women in heaven. The fact that he makes a point of it suggests that some of his contemporaries taught that females would lose all reason to be female once their child-bearing days on earth were over. In that view, femaleness has no value in itself. But if females were not to be

22

females, what would they become? They would be lifted up to the status of males, we may suppose. Thus, only males could inherit the kingdom of heaven. And Augustine did insist that women in heaven would be sexless females. One wonders what kind of dull creature a heavenly sexless female would be. Of course, faith holds the hope that all creation will be changed: all things will be made new. But if sexuality is different in heaven, it will be because it is more, not less, exciting than on earth.

Sexuality is also more basic than child-bearing, but child-conceiving is a happy benefit of our sexuality. It is a most happy combination; sexual intercourse is best between two people who are not trying to avoid children. But if God had created a sexless way of adding children to marriages, he probably would still have made us sexual. Sexuality has its own meaning, its own joys, and its own end. Through sexuality we fulfill ourselves as human beings in union with other human beings. To make reproduction the essence and ultimate goal of sexuality is a put-down of God's creation. But the tie between sexual union and conception of life suggests how deeply the sex act is rooted in humanity. It is the best conceivable combination; but it is not as though sex is only a tool for procreation and not a gift in its own right.

4. SEXUAL PERSONS

I am a male person. I can only vaguely sense how close my maleness comes to my being a person. Very close, I know. My sexuality modifies me as a person; it defines me. I cannot think of myself in any other than male-conscious terms, and I cannot even write this book without maleness showing through along the way. No one else knows me as a person except through my maleness; anyone who knows me at all must know me as a male. Yet my being a person, I sense, is more basic than my being a male. Nobody knows me truly unless he knows me as a person more deeply than as a male. Not even God can separate my maleness from my person; yet somehow I am a person who is *also* male.

Males may assume that their gender will not get in the way of their being treated as persons. Women have often not been granted this assumption. So when women say, "Treat me as a person and not as a woman," one can understand what they want: they want respect for their status as responsible human beings. Religiously, they are demanding respect as equal bearers of God's image. Femaleness is an adjective to personhood. To assign persons roles that they as individuals do not personally choose to accept, and to do this on the basis of gender, is to make sexuality basic and personhood secondary. That evil would be less severe if both sexes were in equal positions to deal out power and privilege. However, the deck is stacked when males grant each other treatment as persons and treat females as merely females.

Of course, when a woman wants to be responded to as a person and *not* as a female, she is asking the impossible. She is defined and her personhood modified too completely by her sexuality. The only way that one could treat her without reference to her own sexuality would be to treat her impersonally. I can communicate with the woman across the counter at my bank without reference to her sex — almost. But I can do this only because I deal with her functionally and not personally; the instant I begin a personal relationship with a woman, I relate to her as male person to a female person.

At the opposite end of the sex-person spectrum, a man could have physical sex with a prostitute who, on that level, would demand that he *not* treat her as a person but only as a female. If he were to try to insinuate himself into her personal life, she would be angry at him for violating their business agreement. What she is selling is the use of her female anatomy, and that is all the buyer has a right to expect. Once intercourse is over, she takes her money and leaves him alone — like a person who sells

24

him a pound of fish. Thus it is possible for a man to relate to a woman in a functional way that does not involve her person: in the case of the bank clerk it involves her femaleness hardly at all; in the case of the prostitute it involves only her female anatomy. In neither case is a man relating to a woman sexually — at least not in any personal sense.

We cannot depersonalize our sex acts without dehumanizing ourselves in some measure. Our sexuality defines our personhood too fully. When a prostitute dissociates herself as a person from her genital action, she is distorting the total unity of her selfhood. So are the husband and wife who go through sexual intercourse without regard for each other's personal needs for affection and concern. But this is a distortion and a failure of human sex. And even when we do so casually, our persons are affected negatively; impersonal sex leaves us less than persons. With respect to personhood and sex it is profoundly true: "What God hath joined together, let not man put asunder."

Our sexuality is the form we take in life as persons. In this sense, sexuality has to do with much more than genital sex. People cannot live by orgasms alone, nor even by exquisitey sensuous love-making. Any two persons who are living a full life together as persons know that their sexual relations cover a lot more ground than the few moments of intercourse. Sexuality is involved in the quiet hours of communication and contemplation as much as in the volcanic moments. The sexploitation of our time is actually a vast shrinkage of sexuality because it concentrates almost wholly on the biological experience of orgasm and everything that stimulates people toward it. The most sensuous person ultimately discovers that the earth-shaking orgasm is not the key to sexual fulfillment. (Though it is also true that failure to achieve orgasm can thwart it.) Sexual bunglers who are groping awkwardly and timidly toward sexual freedom within committed love are growing toward sexual fulfillment that the sensuous virtuoso may never know. Sexual fulfillment is achieved when a personal relationship underpins the genital experience, supports it, and sustains a human sexual relationship after it.

CHAPTER THREE

Distorted Sexuality

Christians must forever pick their way between delight in creation's gifts and sorrow for sin's distortions. We want to rejoice in everything God has given; we want to change all that has gone wrong. Our problem is that we are often hard put to tell the difference between what God has made and what we or nature have bungled. Human expressions of sexuality take on the shapes of many kaleidoscopes, and we cannot always be sure whether we are looking at a sinful distortion or only something strange and vaguely unpleasant to us. In this chapter, I will select a few — and only a few — aspects of sexuality that, as I view them, offer examples of tragic and sometimes comic distortions of sexuality.

Distortions of human sexuality are not quite the same thing as sinful sexual acts. For instance, heterosexual copulation is not a distortion, but it may be a sexual wrong if the two people are not married. Transsexuality may be a distortion of sexuality, but the transsexual person may not at all be guilty of sexual sin. In the latter part of this book, I will talk about moral responsibility in matters of sexual behavior. In this chapter, I will be talking more about sexual inclinations, impulses, and conditions. We cannot separate them completely, but I think the gist of my concern will become clear as we go.

In this same vein, we should keep in mind the difference between sin and tragedy. There is a lot of tragedy in human sexual life, but those who suffer it are not always responsible for it. People are often victims of conditions beyond their control. And if we are to see real people — including ourselves — with a compassionate eye, we must be as sensitive to tragedy as we are to blame. To take an extreme example, a boy born without a penis is a victim of nature's caprice; while he suffers from biological and sexual distortion, he is surely not to be blamed. However, it may be more difficult for many of us to accept innocence when we or others are victims of psychic distortions inflicted on us by the folly of our parents. People are victimized by others, and they carry the burden of their sexual distortions through life with no fault of their own. Since we cannot pinpoint the exact measure of responsibility people have for sexual distortions, we do best to leave precise moral scorekeeping with God. I believe that this is extremely important for Christian people, not only to prevent needless moral judgment of others but also to avoid needless guilt within ourselves.

I want also to remind the reader that our concern, nonetheless, is sexual morality. Our job is to *evaluate* offbeat ways in which our sexuality comes to expression; it is not to probe into the psychic dynamics of how people come by them. I am not going to be discussing the psychology of sexual abnormality. Still, I will have to do some labeling and describing, and the reader is going to have to take my labels and descriptions at face value. I have checked them out with experts in the field and I think they are accurate. But each reader will have to judge for himself whether my labels fit. We must set up some simple norms for our judgments. We are entering a field where angels fear to tread: it is a terrain so variable that nobody can draw a clear map of it. But we must have some standard of sexual normality if we are to talk intelligently about its distortions.

28

For many people, sexual distortions are nauseating. This is the way, for example, many people make judgments on homosexuality. But nausea is not a moral judgment. When a person is shocked or offended by sexual peculiarities, he may only be registering a fact about his tastes. For other people, sexual distortions are what most people do *not* do. That makes it simply a matter of statistics: being abnormal or distorted sexually is simply to be in a minority. But statistics are not the criterion of morality; we cannot get at moral judgments by taking a census. A distortion is a distortion even if ninety percent of the population is involved in it.

By normal expressions of sexuality I have in mind some normative notions. God intends human sexuality to develop along a pattern fitting the truly human life. Within his intention there are opportunities for a rich variety of individual experiences. But there are also some broad but recognizable lines. I think we can locate three normative patterns for our sexual lives: everything in this chapter will be discussed in the light of these.

1. The sexuality of every person is meant to be woven into the whole character of that person and integrated into his quest for human values.

2. The sexuality of every person is meant to be an urge toward and a means of expressing a deep personal relationship with another person.

3. The sexuality of every person is meant to move him toward a heterosexual union of committed love.

The first norm is broken when physical sex is severed from the rest of a person's life as a human being: from his mind and will, from his social self, from his total moral and spiritual selfhood. When it is shoved into a compartment of its own, isolated from a living bond with his other needs and goals, sexuality is an abnormal experience. The second norm is broken when physical release of sexual tension becomes a constant, self-centered goal, when contact with another person is only body contact, and when another person is used like a sex machine to provide sensual pleasures. The third norm is broken when one's sexual inclinations lead him into affairs that tend either to abort or ignore the possibilities of permanent heterosexual commitment. Let us consider some cases.

1. SENSUALISM

Sensuous and sensual pleasure is good, and our desire for it is certainly not a distortion. Our senses are doorways to a world of pleasant experiences; and the world around us is profuse in the smells, sounds, and sights that bring intense pleasure to our lives. They make life rich, intense, and varied. To accept and delight in the sensuous is to be enraptured by the gifts of God. To deny ourselves sensuous pleasure is no virtue: it is to spurn God's splendid creation of things that smell, that sound, and that feel very good; it flattens the splendidly uneven contours of life. The bodies of other people offer wonderful opportunities for sensual pleasure. Our sexuality makes us excitingly sensitive to physical delights in the intimate touching of another person's body. God has made us body-persons finely tuned to pleasure. So, when we talk of sensualism as a distortion of sexuality, it is not the experience of, nor the desire for, sensual pleasure that is suspect.

Sensualism becomes a distortion of sexuality when it cuts physical pleasure in sex off from a personal quest for higher values. It distorts sexuality into a lust for physical pleasure that dominates one's sexual life. Sliced away from one's total growth into a human being of character, sensual pleasure tends to control our sexual development. When it does, it is no longer coordinate with the larger complex of values and hopes that we seek in order to fulfill our lives in company with God and other people. The physical pleasure in sex is no longer received as a bonus, a luxury, a surface enrichment of sexual relationships, but turns into a monster that demands to be the chief purpose of sexual expression. Then sensual pleasure is not part of the rich décor that adds luster to our sexual relationships; it is instead the driving demand and dominating impulse.

All erotic relationships between a man and woman have a sensual dimension even if they never end in bedroom sex. But when the sensual side dominates — when it is pursued separately from the other dimensions — it is distorted into sensualism. The harm of sensualism is, first of all, its effect on the person himself: it hurts deeply just because sexuality is interwoven into his whole being. When a person is dominated by the sensual aspect, which is meant to be a beautiful fringe benefit and not the basic reason for sexuality, everything else in his life is thrown into imbalance. Other values in life have no influence on his sexual life because the sensual is cut off from them. Thus life becomes chaotic because sensual pleasure, though it can control a person, can give no direction. A sensualist is driven but is going nowhere in particular — except in pursuit of the pleasure carrot that always stays at the end of the stick; he is dragged along in every direction that promises a satisfying nibble. And so he aborts the development of his life into personal wholeness because sensualism cannot provide a cohesive center. Only love can. And the sensualist does not know how to let his sexuality lead him into love.

The other harm sensualism does is to rob other people of their basic dignity as body-persons. When the sensualist thinks he engages in sexual relations, he is really only using the body of the other person: he ignores the person and exploits the body as a pleasure machine. The sensual potential of another person's body in contact with his own is all that matters. There is no spiritual mystery, no reaching out for a share in the other's depths, no groping for personal communion — only the desire for the pleasures of body experience. The sensualist distorts sexual experience because he isolates one minor theme and tries to make it the whole symphony. And so he debases the person from whom he seeks pleasure; he does not let her become a partner. He only uses her as an instrument.

Sensualism results when we cop out from the search for a loving, risking, and responsible sharing of communion with another person. It isolates sensual pleasure, and instead of accepting it as an added gift, it makes pleasure the goal of an egotistic, body-centered lunge. Thus one loses the deeper pleasure that sexuality offers, the joy, delight, and ecstasy in communion with another person. This is why sensualism leaves one empty, unsatisfied, always restless for another plunge into the pleasure market. Luxurious as a fringe benefit, physical pleasure in sex becomes banal when it is the only goal of sex. In any other area of life, a desire for sensuous pleasure can be cut off from the rest of one's living without great disaster. But the pleasure of sex cannot be found without the search for communion, because our sexuality needs to infiltrate all the regions of our personalities before it can be fulfilled.

The tragedy of sexual sensualism is compounded by the fact that sensualists are rarely motivated by desire for pleasure alone. The pleasure search is often a disguised search for personal security. A boy who pets with one girl after another is seldom looking only for pleasure from fondling a girl's body; he is unconsciously looking for assurance of his own power as a human being. A middle-aged philanderer is often looking for assurance that he is attractive, virile, desirable. A promiscuous woman needs reassurance that she is lovable, desirable, exciting, womanly. Sensualism, then, is compounded with hidden needs — for power, for domination, or for a sense of self-assurance and worth. A man tries to assure himself, but in his fear of being unworthy to be loved he supports his shaky ego by proving himself a conquering stud in bed. A woman tries to reassure herself, but in her fear of being unworthy to be loved she supports her shaky ego by offering a ready vagina. Sensualism, then, is often a failure to love because of a suspicion that one is unworthy of being loved.

It is easy to say that our epidemic of sensualism is simply the result of crass perversity. But I suspect that it is partly the fault of well-meaning moral people who themselves have stuck sensuous pleasure off in a dark chamber of lower life. Parents who wanted children to grow up properly, with high ideals and noble characters, were often hard put to allow a place within these characters for sensual sex. So young people grew up thinking that the inescapable desire for pleasure was somehow ignoble and unworthy of good persons. Now, as a reaction to that distortion, sensualism has come back with a vengeance. But while we loudly affirm its delights, we still don't know how to integrate it into the rest of our values and goals. And since we do not know how to incorporate it into the broader regions of our characters, we exploit it on the side. Thus, even moral people become part-time sensualists.

2. LOSS OF SHAME

The first thing that must be said about shame is that it is a good thing. Shame is a painful feeling that we are not the persons we ought to be: to be ashamed is to have a sense of our fractured lives, a longing to be whole. To rid ourselves of shame is to lunge into make-believe: for to be without shame is to live in the illusion that we are all we ought to be. I think this must be said, for in our time we are hell-bent on purging ourselves of shame.

Shame became a part of human experience after the Fall. It was a feeling of what is inappropriate for human beings in the fallen life. It is closely linked with sexuality because sexuality is deeply woven into the texture of our very beings. But shame itself can be distorted. It can give false signals that make us feel pain when we should feel none. So, after the Fall, shame came into our lives to make us *feel* the truth of our condition; but in our fallen confusion shame itself is often misplaced.

There are two situations in which people feel no shame. The first is in a state of wholeness. The other is in a state of illusion. In Paradise, we are told, "the man and his wife were both naked, and were not ashamed" (Gen. 2:25). A man and a woman played and worked together as persons whose lives were totally inter-meshed on all levels. Their sexuality was integrated into their entire life. They looked at each other and each saw a person in whom he/she was wholly involved as a helper fit for the other. They had no shame because they had no sense of being anything but what they ought to be: body-persons in loving partnership. They did not "feel" naked because they never felt a need for clothes; nakedness was appropriate to a situation in which people felt no gap between what they were and what they ought to be. In a state of wholeness, there is no shame. After the Fall, "the eyes of both were opened, and they knew that they were naked. . . ." The writer does not specifically say they were ashamed; but we can suppose that "knowing" they were naked was a form of shame. That is, they had a painful feeling that nakedness was no longer appropriate. Why did they have this feeling? They must have felt chagrin at their nakedness in each other's presence because their fellowship as loving partners was broken when they began to accuse each other. This is not a judgment that all nakedness is wrong; but it is a sign that modesty is appropriate in a fallen world.

We become self-conscious when we feel there is something inappropriate about ourselves. I have dreamt on occasion that I appeared as the preacher in a huge church wearing only my underwear. I felt something like shame. At the beach, wearing swimming trunks, I do not have this painful awareness of being without pants. It is a matter of appropriateness. Adam and Eve, in their new awareness that their partnership had broken down, became conscious of their nakedness because they felt it was no longer appropriate for their sexual organs to be exposed in a broken relationship.

The Bible focuses on nakedness because sexuality is very close to what we are as body-persons. Once the togetherness of Adam and Eve had been wholly personal: their maleness and femaleness was experienced within the whole range of their personal lives together. After the Fall they built a wall of suspicion and judgment between themselves. After this, deep personal unity between male and female would be extremely difficult to achieve. Physical and spiritual sex would be constantly splitting apart from each other. Relationships in which the two dimensions of sex were interwoven in a total unity of persons would always be imperfect and incomplete. When Adam and Eve first sensed that their partnership was marred, they became aware of each other as bodies separate from persons. And so the sense of shame came in. Nakedness was not evil; but it was felt as inappropriate for broken personal conditions in a fallen world.

So God gave them clothes to wear: "they sewed fig leaves together and made themselves aprons." The protective impulse of shame led them to put on clothes.

Clothes are appropriate to everyday life in a fallen world. For we are no longer naturally able to see each other as body-persons. We have an inclination, sexually, to see each other as mere bodies, as objects that can be used for genital sex. So we have shame's impulse to cover our genitals. Nakedness is now appropriate only between two people for whom love is restored whole, where physical sex and spiritual sex are interwoven in a union of body-persons.

Our culture tends to misuse God's gift of shame in two ways: on the one hand, we try desperately to get rid of shame; on the other, we exaggerate shame. Our age has been trying to overcome shame in our toleration of public nakedness. We have the illusion that by making nakedness public we could restore health and wholeness to sex. But we have done just the opposite: we have made sex banal, empty, and superficial. Pornography is harmful, among other reasons, because it makes sex trivial, uninteresting, and dull. The worst thing that can happen to sex now is to empty it of mystery, wonder, and longing. The superficial loss of shame tends to remove physical sex from the personal dimension of life, and by doing this removes its mystery and excitement.

However, the world's desire for a shameless society has been a reaction against exaggerated shame; and healthy shame is distorted when we feel ashamed of our sexuality. To feel that one is not what he ought to be because of his sexual longings is to feel ashamed of what God called good. Shame of one's sexuality is destructive of sexuality because a person cannot thus relate to others as persons in a free and wholesome way. His shame makes him fear that every personal feeling he has toward a person of the opposite sex must be a form of lust. It makes him fear that a desire to be close to a woman must be a desire to seduce her. It also hinders the joy of sexual union within marriage: one cannot be glad about a personal-physical union if he is ashamed of the impulses that led him to seek it. Shame often causes people to lead horrible sexual lives. Thus, in terms of consequences, exaggerated shame is a counterpart to loss of shame.

3. IDOLATRY

It is simple to make an idol: slice one piece of created reality off the whole and expect miracles from it. The miracles may be positive or negative; they may heal or hurt. If the idol has power to heal, you keep it around you; you touch it, kiss it, rub it, or manipulate it any way you can. If the idol threatens you, you place a taboo on it, which means that you do not touch it, do not even mention it, for fear that familiarity will have a hurtful backlash. Idols work both ways: we make an idol of something either by expecting too much good from it or by fearing evil from it. Making an idol of sex happens both ways. We make an idol of sex by first isolating one dimension of sexuality — the genital.

Then we either expect everything from it that we need to be happy or we fear that it will hurt us. Either way, sex has become an idol.

One harmful illusion is that if we find the one sexual partner made in heaven for us, our genital experience will bring heaven on earth. Of course, this places a burden on genital sex that nothing, not even the most ecstatic orgasm in history, can bear. Besides, it turns the act of sexual intercourse into an anxious, grasping experience. How can you be sure that your partner is giving you everything you really need or might want? Or how can you be sure that you are providing your partner with his/her great expectations? The biblical statement about the folly of trusting idols is an apt warning about illusions concerning sex. But the idolatry of sex can also occur when we treat it as a taboo. We do this when we are afraid that if it is touched or talked about freely it will harm us: "Talking about sex is putting garbage in the living room." When these notions prevail, sex has been turned into an idol with power to hurt us if we get familiar with it.

Taboo, however, is not the same as reserve. Keeping things in perspective is not the product of fear but of good taste. Nor is talking about sex a cure-all for our sexual problems. People have talked about sex the last several years as they have talked about little else. And we are as far from sexual health as ever — maybe further. In any event, we make an idol of sex in both ways: the impossible expectations and the fearsome flight from sex.

4. THE SEXUAL PUTDOWN

For centuries men have put women down and thus distorted the basic assumption of good sexual relationships. At some point males decided that being female was inferior to being male. Anyone who reads the Old Testament knows that women in the Hebrew community lived in the shadow of men, that they were bit-players in the covenant program, fulfilling their role mainly as incubators for male offspring. Men in the Old Testament community treated women as property to be protected and disposed of at male discretion. We were taught in Sunday school about Jacob's great love for Rachel; but we never stopped to wonder why Rachel had to be bought like a piece of land. Violating a virgin was not a sin against a girl but against her father: to despoil a virgin made her less valuable as dowry bait and more likely to be an unmarried burden on the hands of a father. Existing in the arena where God's program of redemption was unfolding, leading finally to a community where femaleness and maleness were irrelevant to equality and oneness in Christ, the Old Testament folk-morality participated in the antifemale bias of the people around it. This is, of course, not the whole story. The average Hebrew husband loved his wife as devotedly as any modern husband loves his. But private love was practiced in a relationship of gross inequality.

The putdown by male arrogance is complicated by a corresponding male exaltation of female*ness*. Males have sometimes deified femaleness while pushing real live females into second-class status. "Miss America," the sex goddess of American culture, was given her spurious role by a male-dominated society that demanded girl*ness* as a mythological symbol. Reduced now to a Playmate, she is still what males "hunger and thirst after." In medieval times, the deification of femaleness took shape in the cult of the holy virgin. In ancient times, it was the use of the female for influencing the gods at the shrine of sacred prostitution. In early Christianity, the female was often in the opposite direction: the source of all earthly evil, the original temptress, the seductive power that led a good man wrong. Somehow, the male has always managed to extract femaleness from real live women, exalting or degrading the female while ignoring the real person. Femaleness has been set on a pedestal in the shrine of male desire, but real women are relegated to subordinate functionaries in the shadow of the male.

The double standard for sexual morality is another symptom of the putdown. When people view sexuality as a necessary evil, they usually make allowances for the myth that males are naturally polygamous and females naturally monogamous, that male sexuality is aggressive and female sexuality passive. Males are thus granted grudging immunity from the ethic of abstinence before marriage and fidelity within marriage. The male-dominated society tolerated the man's rampant need for sexual release, while it demanded purity and virginity on the part of his bride. The resulting obvious risks of promiscuity for the woman have, until the development of the contraceptive pill, made sexual freedom more hazardous for the woman than for the man — though, morally, this is beside the point. The willingness of women to go along with the double standard is only a testimony to how thoroughly they have been put down by men.

5. ECCENTRICITY AND DISTORTION

Sometimes sexuality walks a crooked path. We feel ripples of sexual movement that seem odd and even bizarre. In some cases these are no more than sexual oddities; in others they may become grotesque and violent distortions. The difference between an eccentricity and a distortion may sometimes be only in the beholder's eye. At other times the difference is massive and painfully real. But in between we are often left in shameful bewilderment at our own secret inclinations, wondering whether we are perverse or slightly eccentric.

At this point it will be valuable to recall our lines of definition for sexual normality: (1) Sexuality is interwoven with the total character development of a person. (2) Sexuality is a biologically rooted drive toward personal communion. (3) Sexuality is a movement toward heterosexual relations that are climaxed in a committed, loving, and permanent union. Any sexual eccentricity that aborts any of these or is continuously substituted for them is at least the beginning of distortion. But we must also remember that sexual distortions are not necessarily personal sins that need burden us with personal guilt. I do not want to make believe that sexual distortions are always free from sin or are never the wages of sin. But I do think we must make a studied effort not to put guilt labels on people who are in fact suffering victims.

A. Fetishism

Some people are sexually aroused by things that have nothing to do with sex. Things like shoes, gloves, a piece of rubber, or some soft silky cloth can stimulate some people. These things are called fetishes (the word is transferred from its more common meaning: anything that people believe has supernatural power and is therefore treated with great reverence). American males tend to be turned on by breasts; but we would not call the breast a fetish because it seems to be related to sexuality. Chinese men, I understand, are often aroused by a dainty female foot. Americans might think such fascination with a foot a fetish; but a Chinese man might think it intrinsically sexy. So we cannot be absolute. But most of us would agree that a shoe or piece of fur that turns people on would be a fetish.

Now when is a fetish a distortion? In our definition, fetishism is sexual distortion whenever it substitutes for genital relationships. Many of us are turned on sexually by things that leave other people cold; but they may only arouse us to seek sexual relations with our spouses. If a man's wife is aware that some odd object aroused him to make love, she may be offended and hurt. And her *response* to his fetish may make it harder for her to accept him as a sexual partner. At that point, the real moral issue is whether she can believe that her husband loves and wants her, and whether she can tolerate an eccentricity in the husband she loves. But sometimes a fetish becomes a *substitute* for personal sexual relations. Men have been known to have secret passions for brassieres, especially ones they steal. They may collect them, fondle them, and masturbate at the sight of them. Why people develop fetishes is hidden in their own past experiences; we need not get into deep causes. But when a fetish substitutes for a person, it is a profound distortion. When a fetish becomes a sexual object and not a sexual stimulus, it prevents the person from entering the challenge of a real relationship with another person.

The abnormality of fetishism is not very difficult to recognize. Ideally, only a *person* we love should stimulate us sexually. But we must not be perfectionists. If we are *stimulated* to seek personal relations by an impersonal object, we will do well not to be plagued by our eccentricity. But if an impersonal object substitutes for a person, we will do well to face our abnormality, seek its cause, and accept help to overcome it.

B. Masochism

Masochism involves receiving pleasure from pain. To get sexual pleasure from pain sounds like a morbid distortion of sexuality, and it often is. But masochism is not a simple condition. In sexual experience, pain is almost always blended into pleasure. No one can separate the two. Shakespeare spoke of "the lover's pinch which hurts and is desired." In some places, scratch scars on one's back are proof of successful sexual action. And there is perhaps a spoonful of masochism in all of us. Harmless masochism is found, however, not only in the pain people feel in sexual encounters; some people are aroused toward sexual relationships by being caused pain. Some wives are aroused when their husbands "play rape" with them. Or a wife may be asked to spank her husband in a sexual ritual and may be profoundly shaken. But she faces a decision. Can she accept eccentricity because she loves the eccentric person? Or will love disappear because she cannot tolerate something she feels to be distorted and sick?

When does the harmless pleasure of pain turn the corner into sickly masochism? What separates the person who desires to be beaten and humiliated from excited lovers moaning in their ecstasy of sexual pain? When does an eccentricity become a self-destructive distortion? The line must be drawn at the point where the desire for pain obstructs a person's passage into creative and responsible relationships of love and tenderness with other persons.

Masochism may take the form of a desire for degrading submission to another person. A sickly masochist's sexual inclinations are controlled by a bizarre wish to be humiliated, punished, mastered, and abused by another person. This is why extreme masochism often takes the form of wishing to be bound and punished. Here a person is not feeling pain *within* a sexual relationship but is experiencing pain as a *substitute* for a sexual relationship. The beating and binding give sexual satisfaction without a sexual relationship. The disorder is not simply in a person's desire for pain: the sexual distortion in masochism lies in its bizarre and self-distinctive substitute of pain and humiliation for interpersonal relationships of love and commitment.

C. Sadism

The masochist needs someone with at least a smidgen of sadism in him to cooperate in the pain game. The sadist, unfortunately, does not need a willing partner. This difference makes the sadist more than an eccentric or even sick person; it makes him very dangerous. But on the lower end of the scale, the tendency to inflict pain in sexual passion is so common that we are hard put even to call it an abnormality. If the most tender lover examines his own impulses, he will discover a controlled desire to bring pain to his partner. Loving bites, hard kisses, forceful thrusts, scratching and pinching — these and other more ingenious ways of causing pain reveal a touch of sadism in sexual inclinations. But they are normally tied up with a desire to bring pleasure at the same time they are giving a bit of pain. And they are controlled by a deep respect for the dignity and integrity of one's partner.

There is, of course, an enormous difference between a slight, seductive sadism, played out in the privacy of marriage and limited to playful skirmishes, on the one hand, and compulsively destructive sadism on the other. The difference is so stark that we use the label "sadism" for both only by stretching language to a breaking point. One difference is that playful sadism between sexual partners is controlled by love; the lover stops when the partner complains. It is also controlled by some inner sensor within the person inflicting pain. However, pathological sadism is marked by lack of both controls. Pain is inflicted not to please but to abuse. And it is compulsive: the sadist is mastered by his own horrible impulse to hurt. Triggered by some unconscious mechanism, the sadist's fury erupts into flaming violence.

Sadism is not always physical. Psychological brutality, the constant putdown by a husband or wife, often silently endured, is a form of sadism — sometimes also uncontrolled and sick. A man can take inverted pleasure in humiliating and abusing his wife without ever putting a hand on her body. A woman can use her sexuality to make a husband feel incompetent and inadequate by subtly beating him down with her sexual demands or sexual rejections. She can make him feel like either a sexual incompetent or a sexual beast; in either case she is punishing him, and this certainly indicates a touch of sadism.

The relationship between sadism and sexuality is a terribly complicated matter that psychologists can only generalize about. A rapist may only use sex in order to abuse and humiliate a person; men who rape for the sake of sex seem to be a minority among rapists. He may use sex as a tool of violence and conquest.

But other sadists seem to get sexual satisfaction in maiming and killing where no genital sex is carried out. We stand at the abyss of a demonic distortion. The very complexity of sadism shows how sexuality permeates many of the nonsexual components of our life: it works out in tenderness and concern, but it can also work out in monstrous hostility and compulsive cruelty. This should tell us that the deepest effects of sin arise not from our glands but from our spirits. It also shows how our sexuality can be demonized by nonsexual forces.

Mild sadism is a larger part of our sexual inclinations than we like to admit. A tinge of sadism can be a tolerable eccentricity if it is controlled; but sadism can also be a distortion that flames up into orgies of savagery. I have used both terms — masochism and sadism — for a wide range of experiences. Ordinarily we use these labels only for extreme or pathological cases. But I have used them loosely for a reason: we must recognize that these distortions are only a fuzzy fathom away from some of our normalities. Let each person attend to his own impulses.

D. Transvestism and Transsexuality

Here we have two sexual oddities that have something in common but are very different in their effects on the people involved. A transvestite is a person who likes to wear the clothes and mimic the manners of the opposite sex; a transvestite does *not* think he/she is the other sex. A transsexual person *does* feel like and want to be the other sex. The line between them is not always clear, but there is a difference. I am going to suggest that transvestism is a sexual eccentricity and that transsexuality is a distortion. But I want to emphasize that a person may be no more at fault morally for a sexual abnormality than he would be for having a broken nose.

Nature is not one hundred percent reliable. A male baby

may be born with the proper male chromosomes but with an undeveloped male sex apparatus. Now and then a newborn male has been mistaken for a female because his penis never matured in the fetal stage. What happens to this person's feelings when he later discovers that he is a boy after all? In other cases, where nature works properly mothers function very badly. A woman may have a son but want a daughter; she may want the daughter so strongly, and she may hate men so thoroughly, that she feels a compulsion to treat her boy as if he were a girl. She may dress him up in girl's clothing, play mother-daughter games with him, and give him special praise for whatever he does that makes him seem like a girl. And he learns to take pleasure — to be reinforced, as we now say — in his girlishness because of the pleasure he gives to his male-hating mother. Thus, sometimes biology and sometimes mixed-up parents can shove a child toward either transvestite eccentricity or transsexual abnormality.

A transvestite is a person who violates his *own* notions of how a male or female should dress and act. He needs to dress or act as he supposes only the other sex does. He does not want to be the other sex; he wants to be a male or female who occasionally *acts* like the other sex. And in doing so he receives some sexual titillation. His needs will probably create trouble for him when he relates to real persons: when a male transvestite's wife first discovers that he is turned on by wearing her clothes, he is in trouble. So is his wife. Transvestism becomes a moral question at this point: will it prevent a good heterosexual relationship? If so, will he be willing to get therapy to understand and overcome his needs, or will he suppress them and bury them underground where they will do even more harm? This is his moral challenge. Transvestism is not immoral, but what one does with it is a moral issue. Of course, if his wife can transcend her shock, love him with his oddities, and not brand him as a pervert, his problem can be their private sexual joke. And he may then be on the way to shedding his odd need.

There are a few people who not only like to act out the roles of the other sex but want to *be* the other sex. We call these people transsexuals. In a way, they feel they are the other sex; only their anatomy does not match what they feel they are in their souls. A person with male sex organs may have been reared like a girl, or perhaps something went wrong with his hormonic balance. (Since it is impossible to keep our pronouns straight, I will use male pronouns to refer to both sexes.) In any case, he feels like and wants to be a girl; he hates his genitalia. So sometimes he goes the route of surgery to remove his penis and implant a vagina, and he takes estrogens to develop female breasts. He cannot have babies, but otherwise he becomes a woman capable of sexual relations with a man. The reverse situation is true for the female transsexual.

What is the moral problem here, if any? Clearly, what nature and God intended to be one sex turns out to be experienced as the other sex; so it is an abnormality. But we can be sure that no one would consciously choose to enter this agonizing experience. Transsexuals are victims either of biological accident or childhood abuse, and in either case their abnormality is morally innocent. But is the decision to exchange male for female genitals a moral issue? It is certainly an extremely crucial decision. Removing healthy genitals and replacing them with the genitals of the other sex does not seem to have the same purely medical consequences as amputating a gangrenous arm or leg. We are sensitive about mutilating sexual organs because we sense their closeness to what we are as sexual persons. Therefore, to many people it appears to be a perverse meddling with one's created being to contrive a conversion of one's sexuality. But this is an oversimplified reaction on the part of those who cannot project into a transsexual person's tragedy. Is it worse to use surgery to match a person's external sexuality with his inner sexuality, or to live as a male soul within a female body? We must remember that a transsexual — as far as we can tell — did not choose to be what he is. Someone or something pushed his soul in the direction of the opposite sex. Why then should he not choose to have his body adjusted to the soul of that opposite sex which someone else gave him?

But this too is somewhat oversimplified. We must ask whether the surgery will give the transsexual the possibility of a good heterosexual relationship. Obviously, the situation is risky. No male body can be converted to a child-producing female body. Thus one ingredient of a heterosexual relationship will always be missing. Further, the law has not caught up with science. Marriage between a transsexual who had become a female and a normal male has been annulled on the legal ground that the wife was really a man. Further, while the converted male transsexual may be capable of functioning sexually as a female, the partner will have a difficult time relating easily to someone who once was male and only through transplanted organs has become female. So the prospects for a deep personal relationship are not bright. But we must still ask whether this is worse than living as a female within a male body or a male within a female body. And this is a question that can be answered only by the transsexual person.

We could also ask whether there is an alternative to surgery. Since it is the soul that has become alien to the body, perhaps the transsexual ought rather to have his soul reconditioned. That is, since nature gave him a male body, he is clearly "intended" to be a male. Therefore, perhaps he ought to try to be healed inwardly, to bring his soul in line with creation's real intent. Perhaps psychiatric therapy could bring his feelings in tune with his genitals. But there is a hitch here. The male transsexual is a person who feels like, wants to be, and, in his view, is a female (or vice versa). And since wanting to change is the basic requirement for change, the transsexual is a very poor candidate for therapy.

At this point we will do well to leave moral judgment with God and accept the transsexual as a victim of nature's whim or humanity's folly. The normal sexual community ought to accept its task of loving concern for the transsexual person, admire the courage it took to undergo surgery, and put its resources at his/her service for the best possible adjustment to what must be an uncertain and hard future.

6. HOMOSEXUALITY

As I begin this section, I am aware that anything said about the morality of homosexuality in such a brief space will be superficial. It will be misunderstood by Christian heterosexuals as flabby concession and by homosexuals as unfeeling intolerance. I am willing to take the risk partly because any chapter on sexual distortions simply must take account of homosexuality. And, besides, I do have a sense of urgency about some things that ought to be said. My word to heterosexual people is that we must assess homosexuality with humility, compassion, and sober moral judgment. My word to homosexuals is that they, like everyone else, are called to be morally responsible in their decision about what to do with their homosexuality. With this modest purpose, we can perhaps say something useful even though we say nothing complete.

We who are heterosexual need to exercise humility when we talk about homosexuality simply because we are very ignorant. Most of us can only guess what it is like to be homosexual. In fact, not even homosexual people are experts; their sexuality is a mystery to them just as heterosexuality is a mystery to most straight people. It is stupid to suppose that we can get clear information on homosexuality from homosexual people: their understanding of their sexuality is just as limited as heterosexuals' understanding of theirs. They may be experts on what they suffer, but they are not necessarily experts on what they are.

The label "homosexual" can be used for a wide variety of human experience. Young people often feel strong affection for friends of their own sex; some actually go through a brief homosexual phase without realizing it, and then go on to happy heterosexual lives. Adults often have feelings inside them that churn up fears about their sexual identity; many people have felt tremors of homosexual impulse and dare not admit it even to themselves. Some people move in and out of both sexual worlds, never knowing for sure where they really belong. Others get involved in homosexual practices for a while — in the army or in prison, for instance — and then return easily to a heterosexual life. A fairly small number of people (about 5% of the male and 2½% of the female population) grow into maturity totally confirmed in a sexual drive toward people of their own sex. We call them "constitutional homosexuals." But even these people vary as much in their drives, their life-styles, and their moral values as do heterosexual people.

So when we talk about homosexuality we are talking about a wide variety of experiences. But even if we locate the common denominator in some consistent inclination toward sexual relations with people of the same sex, we are talking about a mystery. We don't know for sure why some people have these inclinations; moreover, we don't know for sure what sorts of inclinations they are. Is the attraction purely physical? The homosexual person vigorously denies that his sexual relationships are merely genital. All we know about for sure is that the homosexual *behavior* is abnormal. But that tells us little about the personal dimensions of the homosexual condition. Let it just be said, then, that no matter how sure some heterosexual people are in their moral judgments, they make them in a fog of ignorance about the deeper goings on in a homosexual's life.

We who are heterosexual must show compassion because we are not talking about strange, subhuman, and monotonously stereotyped creatures; we are talking about persons who are as different from one another as heterosexual people are. We are talking about images of God. And, especially, we are talking about people whose sexual life is often a journey into anxiety and loneliness. A homosexual is anxious because he suspects that homosexual relationships offer little promise of deep and lasting fulfillment. He is lonely because he has to struggle with his sexual identity among people who cannot understand and whose social institutions have no place for him. Most homosexual people do not spend their evenings hanging around gay bars in search for sympathy and sex. Thousands of homosexual people live highly moral and often deeply religious existences. They must grope their way painfully into a creative and useful life amid a community of people who — try as they will — cannot fully sympathize with their struggle. So we, for whom even heterosexual adjustment is often painful, ought at least to be compassionate in whatever moral judgments we make about homosexual people. Finally, we must resolve to form reasoned judgments because we tend easily to let either sentiment or nausea crowd out critical appraisal of homosexual abnormalities. We have to find our way between two common and simple conclusions:

1. Homosexuality is simply a special form of normal sexuality. A homosexual person is different only because he happens to be in a minority. He is following his God-given nature just as a heterosexual is following his, and he looks for the same deep personal experience in sexual relations that any normal person does. There is no reason for him to change or want to change his inclinations. If there is a moral problem in connection with homosexuality, it lies with heterosexuals who in their ignorance and arrogance deprive homosexual people of their rights to full equality in society.

2. Homosexuality is a self-chosen perversion. The homosexual person is a decadent and dangerous creature. He is not simply sick in any medical sense; he is unhealthy and abnormal in a moral sense. He simply wills to distort nature and corrupt others in the process. His only decent course is to will to change his evil inclinations and to choose to become a heterosexual. If he does not change, it is only because he prefers degeneracy to

50

normality. Being a degenerate, he is a menace to weak hetero-sexuals. So, if he does not change his nauseating ways, society must coerce him.

The first view is the judgment of sentiment; the second is a judgment of revulsion. Both are superficial. Neither is a re-sponsible approach to the total problem. How can we come to a judgment that is realistic and Christian, while we judge in humil-ity and compassion? In the Bible we get a clear and certain message: it tells us that homosexual practices are unnatural and godless. There can be no doubt about this. The Old Testament outlawed homosexual behavior and demanded the head of any-one caught in it (Lev. 18:22; 20:13).

We realize, of course, that the Mosaic Law has some other interesting sexual rules: for instance, any male who tragically loses his sexual organs in an accident forfeits the privilege of entering the sanctuary (Deut. 23:2). And a married couple caught (by whom?) having sex during the wife's menstrual period is ostracized (Lev. 20:18). We need some interpreter's rule for selecting one law as a moral norm and the other as cultic fussiness; yet most people feel secure in sensing that homosexual acts are not on the same level with the other sexual offenses. The New Testament is just as intolerant of homosexual practices as is the Old Testament. Along with other less reprehensible doings, homosexual acts disqualify a person for the kingdom of God (I Cor. 6:9-10). The clinching indictment comes in Paul's description of what happens to human life when God abandons it to its own devices: "For this reason God gave them up to dishonorable passions. Their women exchanged natural relations for unnatural, and their men likewise gave up natural relations with women and were consumed with passion for one another . . ." (Rom. 1:26). When God lets people go, ho-mosexual depravity is one of the intolerable upshots.

I have no reason to doubt that Paul is right. But I do wish that we had a clearer grasp of why homosexuality is unnatural. The notion of unnaturalness is strong in Paul's judgment, and I suppose many heterosexuals also feel comfortable with Calvin's words: "homosexuals," he said, "have become worse than beasts, since they have reversed the whole order of nature." On the other hand, we should take the trouble to notice that Paul also believed long hair on men to be unnatural (I Cor. 11:14). Nature does not speak as clearly to me about long hair as it did to Paul, but long hair and homosexuality are hardly in the same category. So we should ask *in what respect* homosexuality distorts nature? Thomas Aquinas pinpointed its distortion as sex without the possibility of conception. But many heterosexuals today have sex without the intention to procreate, and not many of us brand this as a reversal of the whole order of nature.

I think it may be useful to think back to our three norms for normal (natural) development of sexuality. What we want to do is lift our judgment of what is natural above judgments based on statistics or personal taste. That is, we want more to go on than the fact that most people are heterosexual and that many heterosexuals are nauseated by homosexuality. The three norms are again: (1) Human sexuality ought to be integrated into the total development of a person's character. (2) Human sexuality ought to tend toward expression in personal relationships. (3) Human sexuality ought to drive us toward permanent hetero-sexual union.

Obviously, homosexuality violates the third norm. And here the basic issue is joined. The homosexual advocate simply denies that heterosexual union is normative. So where does this leave us? It seems utterly clear to me that the Bible from beginning to end views the heterosexual union as God's intention for sexuality. From the beginning "he made them male and female" so that they might become "one flesh." We have here the major assumption of all judgment on homosexuality: *all* human sexuality is intended to be climaxed in heterosexual marriage. Is it true? There is no way to settle this except by a decision of faith that the biblical indicators are indeed true to God's intent.

We may also ask whether homosexuality has any promise for *personal* sexual relationship. Can two homosexual people establish a deeply personal union in which genital sex is one component in a mutual sharing of each other's depth and mystery as persons? The question cannot be answered by a leap from someone's theory of homosexuality. Homosexual people often do seem to relate to each other in deeply personal unions; not every homosexual association is a quick encounter between two gay bar prowlers. But we can ask whether homosexuals have a built-in obstacle to meaningful sexual relations in which physical sex is integrated into a total personal union. In some theories, the homosexual's fear of the opposite sex is more basic than his preference for people of his own sex. A male homosexual's fear of females prevents his sexual life from maturing beyond a boyhood stage. But his physical or genital needs are as demanding as anyone's. So he gets involved with other males genitally, but he relates to them personally on an immature level. His relationships are frequently superficial, focused mainly on genital satisfaction.

This is only a theory. And its conclusion should be matched by the observation that many heterosexual relations are superficial and impersonally genital. Furthermore, homosexual persons sometimes do overcome their handicap and achieve deeply personal associations over a long period of time. Rather than pontificate that homosexuals are doomed to merely physical relations, let us be glad that their relations are often as personally constructive as they can be. We have to say that the second norm for normal sexual development is harder for the homosexual than for the heterosexual — but not impossible.

The first norm is also difficult for the homosexual to live by. The reasons are complex, but the homosexual person has a formidable problem integrating his sexual development as a theme within the symphony of his personal life. It is hard enough for heterosexuals, and perhaps impossible for homosexuals. Early in

53

life he has to deal with his sexuality as something he fears and despises. This may be due to his morally disapproving environment, or it may be due to some deeper intuition that his inclinations are bound to lead him into suffering. He has none of the cultural supports that remind heterosexuals of the beauty and excitement and goodness of their drives. His search for sexual satisfaction often has to be carried on in furtive, treacherous, and often seamy conditions. And, finally, if it is true that he tends to be obsessed with genital sex and not with personal fulfillment, there is no way he can deal with his sexuality as a personal component interwoven through the rest of his values and expectations as a complete human being.

I have tried to isolate three norms for human sexual development. These are, I think, behind what Paul means by natural sexuality. And if they accurately translate the biblical view of the normal drive for sexual expression, we must conclude that Paul was right: homosexuality is "unnatural" — or abnormal, as we more easily say today. This is all I wish to say as a heterosexual's judgment on homosexuality. I need to be reminded, however, as I think every Christian heterosexual does, that our judgment must be made in humility and compassion; if it is not, it is a judgment of arrogance and, to that extent, an un-Christian judgment.

We have been talking of homosexuality as a condition. What of the homosexual person? Again, it is important that we not judge a person because of his homosexual condition. No homosexual, to my knowledge, ever decides to be homosexual; he only makes the painful discovery at one time or another that he is homosexual. We need not go into causes here: whether he is a victim of some freaky upset in his central nervous system, or the victim of a maternal or paternal monster in his nursery, does not really matter as far as we are concerned. He is a product of forces over which he had no control. He merits blame for being homosexual no more than a mentally retarded child does for being retarded.

But what about the homosexual person's responsibility

toward his own life as a homosexual? His life is a gift of grace just as mine is, and he is a steward of his life as I am. What ought he to do with his homosexuality? This too must be asked with enormous compassion. For the obstacles on his route to a moral and happy life are incalculably greater than mine. But painfully vast as his problems are, he is still a person living before God with freedom to choose, within the limits set for him by nature, what he will do with his abnormal sexuality.

Christian moralists, speaking in the twilight of their ignorance, are often amazingly quick to spell out the exact line of duty for the homosexual person. Karl Barth, for instance, felt quite free to lay down one simple mandate for anyone with this "perversion": let him be converted and turn from his decadent way of life. This may be theoretically sound admonition — as long as it is abstracted from real persons. It may not be bad ethical judgment; but it is ineffective pastoral counsel. The confirmed homosexual simply cannot turn by a heroic act of his will. If there are such persons as "constitutional homosexuals," their responsibility toward themselves will have to be viewed with more finesse than a simple command to become heterosexuals, or even to stop being homosexuals.

I would like to outline three steps of what seem to me the ingredients of responsible confrontation with one's own homosexuality.

1. Self-knowledge

a. He should courageously face the abnormality of his condition. There can be no "okay, stay gay" attitude in his own assessment of his homosexuality. He must resist the temptation to say: "This is my nature, so it is normal for me."

b. He should simply refuse to accept a burden of guilt for his condition. He is a victim either of biological accident or someone else's folly. He ought to seek help, if need be, to lift the needless burden of blame he is sorely tempted to bear by himself. He ought to work to overcome the self-doubt and self-hatred that lie beneath his homosexual condition. Here the possibilities of divine grace are open to him; grace can enable him to see himself as God's creature and child of irreducible worth and inestimable potential.

c. He should recognize his own responsibility for what he does with his homosexual drives. While he did not choose homosexuality, he must agonize with the options he has before him once he has faced and acknowledged his homosexual condition.

2. *Hope*

a. He ought to believe that change is possible. Statistics on homosexual conversion are certainly not promising; but no homosexual person can be absolutely sure of what is possible for him. He has no right to be fatalistic.

b. He ought to seek change. The Christian homosexual ought to open himself to the possibility of divine healing. There are too many testimonies to God's help in changing a person's sexual orientation for them to be ignored. Further, he should seek psychiatric help to modify his behavior. He should, for instance, consider whether it might be better to convert *from* homosexuality even if he cannot convert *to* heterosexuality. Again, the statistics are not encouraging, but no individual can be sure it is impossible for him.

In short, given the abnormality of the homosexual condition, a person whose tragic misfortune it is to suffer it is morally responsible to gear his choices in the direction of changing the condition that victimizes his life.

3. *Accommodation*

Let us now assume that "constitutional homosexuality" is real, that a person's sexuality is so deeply conditioned toward homosexual responses that he cannot change. Let us use the word "cannot" with reservations; but we may use it in the sense that change appears extremely unlikely, especially in mature people, and especially after lengthy therapy has been futile. What responsibility does a confirmed homosexual person have? What are his options?

a. *Celibacy.* He ought at least to consider whether his affliction is a call to celibacy. Behavioral modification techniques can be used, if not to convert one to a heterosexual life, at least to modify his behavior away from homosexual practices. Extremely difficult as it is to choose the celibate life, it can be achieved with help. Ordinarily no one has the right to prescribe celibacy for another person. But in view of the judgment that homosexual life is ethically unwarranted and personally unsatisfying, the choice should be very seriously weighed.

b. *Optimum Homosexual Morality.* We must face the possibility that for any homosexual person none of the options we have mentioned is feasible. It is easy for the heterosexual moralist to cut off the discussion at this point and "leave the homosexual person in his sin." But we must follow the homosexual person to the edges of his options. So we also ask, What morality is left for the homosexual who finally — and to the best of his knowledge — can manage neither change nor celibacy? He ought, in this tragic situation, to develop the best ethical conditions in which to live out his sexual life. There must be no exploitation, no seduction, and no enticement of youth into the homosexual sphere. The homosexual ought to keep himself away from vocations where the temptation of seduction is high. He ought to develop the nonsexual sides of his life with intensity, so that the sexual side may at least be kept proportionate to other parts of life. He ought to relate to people of his own sex on a nonsexual level. Within his sexual experience, he ought to develop permanent associations with another person, associations in which respect and regard for the other as a person dominate their sexual relationship.

To develop a morality for the homosexual life is *not* to accept homosexual practices as morally commendable. It is, however, to recognize that the optimum moral life within a deplorable situation is preferable to a life of sexual chaos.

The Christian Community

The responsibility of the Christian community is dual-focused. On the one hand, the church must, if it takes biblical ethics seriously, clearly proclaim the ethical unacceptability of homosexual relationships. It should also make plain the fullness of grace to homosexual persons, not only in reference to their condition but to their acts as well. One important goal of the church's fellowship is the restoration of the homosexual as a person loved by God and of great worth in God's sight; but the only way this can be done is by demonstrating that he is also of great worth in the community's sight. A community of personal acceptance and support is the absolute imperative for any ministry in Christ's name to the homosexual struggling to live a Christian life.

The church should also realistically but hopefully offer the possibility of divine healing; it will make a great mistake if it promises instant conversion, but it will cut off hope for the homosexual if it ignores the possibility. Here, as in few other situations, the church is called on to set creative compassion in the vanguard of moral law. And it must be willing to live with ambivalence. It cannot make believe that the homosexual person is simply a member of a sexual minority group. On the other hand, it cannot fulfill its ministry simply by demanding chastity. It must offer divine hope along with morality.

The agonizing question that faces pastors of homosexual people comes when the homosexual has found it impossible to be celibate. What does the church do? Does it drop its compassionate embrace and send him on his reprobate way? Does it imitate God, as Paul described him in Romans 1:26 — that is, does it abandon him to his unnatural passion? Or does it, in the face of a life unacceptable to the church, quietly urge the optimum moral life *within* his sexually abnormal practice? Does it in effect say, Since you are unable to opt for the better, at least avoid the worst? And does it help him to avoid the worst while it continues to embrace him as a person? These are questions each community must answer for itself.

*   *   *

Threaded through this discussion of sexual distortions are some themes that should be summarized. I wanted to say that the effects of sin on our sexuality are not limited to technical lapses into forbidden acts. Sin infiltrates our sexuality to prevent its development into a truly humane component of life together. The basic fault that has crept into our sexuality is the failure of the mysterious power of biological sex to lead us into the life of love. I have also wanted to say that not every sexual oddity need be considered a sexual distortion: much that is eccentric can be digested by love. There is also the point that not every distortion of sexuality need be condemned in others or judged in oneself as personal failure; much of what we are sexually is not of our doing. It may be a distortion that we can overcome, or it may be one we have to live with. But it is too much to demand that everyone who bears the burden of a sexual failure need in addition bear a burden of guilt. There is, of course, a responsibility that everyone bears — to whatever extent he is capable — of living as humane a life as he can by means of and through his sexuality.

If this were all that could be said about distortions of God's created gift of sexuality, we would be left in despair. Redemption is a hope offered to men and women in their sexuality, and thus human sexuality as well as human spirituality is open to the gift of grace. To that we turn in the chapter that follows.

59

CHAPTER FOUR

Salvation and Sexuality

The gospel of Jesus Christ is good news for the whole person; so the gospel must be good news for us in our befuddled attempts to live with our sexuality. If Christ promises hope, it must include hope for a better sexual life. Our sexuality is woven too thoroughly into the garment of our lives to be left out of life's renewal in Christ. For this reason our relationship to Jesus Christ cannot mean salvation *from* sexuality; nor can it mean only some new rules for the sexual game. We must receive the word of the gospel as the word of grace and freedom. And in doing so we must by all means understand that grace is not against nature but only against distortions of nature. Grace does not put sexuality down; it raises sexuality up into the service of spirit. For this reason the grace of God must be the grace that liberates our sexuality as a power for love.

Yet for many people through the centuries, becoming a Christian has meant a suppression of sexuality. Who knows how many Christian people have suspected that if they were truly Christ-led they would have less truck with the sexual side of life? This chapter is meant for such people. I hope it will offer them at least some insight into the positive role that sex can play in their lives as Christian persons. What I want to do in this chapter is suggest some aspects of New Testament Christianity that form the spiritual context for our sexual lives. I am not going to discuss the Christian do's and don't's of sexual behavior here. I will be talking instead about the new spiritual environment for sexual behavior.

1. BODY-LIFE AFFIRMED

"The Word became flesh." This is the gospel's absolute yes to human sexuality. God's romance with humankind includes his becoming one with us all the way. What bothered many Christian believers from the outset was just this aspect of the incarnation; not divine logistics, but divine decency. Many early Christians had no special problem believing that God *could* become man; their problem was a matter of taste: it seemed improper that a holy God *would* take a human body. People were offended by the incarnation, especially, because of their low view of the vital and spontaneous element of sexuality in the human body. But the faith of the church saved the day for the biblical message that God became man like us in all things, but without sin.

The body of Jesus, Christians believe, was a real earthy body of tissue and bones, glands and hormones. Jesus' body had the same goings-on inside it that ours do. Christian piety does not have to be nervous about the sexuality of Jesus. He was a male, and his masculinity shaped his human life from his hormones to his soul. God did not become a third sex; he did not become neuter. He became a male and lived among women and men as a male. It is true that Jesus did not get married, and this fact tells us something about the possibilities of being a sexual human being without having genital sexual relationships. It is true that the biological movement of sexuality leads in the direction of sexual intercourse. But it is also true that sexuality is not defined by a penis's penetration of a vagina, but by the broadest range of male and female responses to each other. And it seems true, likewise, that the drive toward genital sex experience can be rechanneled. The life of Jesus, in all his human relationships and especially in his transcending mission to seek and to save the lost, demonstrates the possibility of being sexual without experiencing genital sex.

Jesus did not experience genital sex. But this need not mean that he had no feeling of being a man among women. The differences between male and female did not melt into a vague mass called human nature when he looked at real men and women. He related to women as a male to females. He must have felt the difference between the tender touch of women and the hard handclasp of men. And there is no reason to suppose that he had no erotic feelings toward women, that he never enjoyed the sheer female presence of Mary. Nor is there any reason to suppose that women felt no erotic attraction toward him. "I don't know how to love him," sang Mary in *Jesus Christ Superstar.* Naturally! She had known "love" only in terms of genital sex. Now, for the first time, a male was calling depths of personal passion out of her that she did not know she had. How was a sexually turned-on woman to know, at first encounter, what to do about the male Jesus? She had to learn how to love him.

He was, we read, tempted in all points as we are. But Christians have seldom been able to imagine that Jesus was even inclined to make love with a woman. Why are pious feelings offended at this thought? Does it seem horrid because we have a sneaking suspicion that sex is unworthy of the Savior of men — and is it unworthy of him because it is really unworthy of us? We may be sure that if Jesus was inclined, he did not think of it as a temptation to do evil. For Jesus, an urge toward sexual love would be in the same category as a temptation to take up fishing for a living or to lead a revolt against the Roman occupation forces. Neither of these would be a temptation to do evil;

both would be a temptation to turn away from his supreme vocation.

What Jesus did for human sexuality was considerable. For instance, he treated women as persons equal with men. Running bluntly against both Jewish and Gentile culture, he publicly displayed a tenderness and concern for women that demonstrated his respect for them as persons. He accepted them in his inner circle of friends. He turned against the legalistic double standards of his time by exposing the hypocrisy of the males who accused a woman caught in adultery. He undermined legalistic morality by recalling that the heart has its own kind of sex life. He subverted male arrogance by contradicting the Jewish tradition that approved of the exclusive right of husbands to get rid of their wives as they got rid of their stock. He showed that marriage and sex were planted in the Garden of Eden, reminding us that God intended from the beginning that men and women should be sexually attracted toward each other, and that sexuality therefore was not one of the nasty products of sin but the exciting dynamic of creation (Mark 10:5-9).

Jesus did not have to talk about sexuality to affirm it. Sexuality is affirmed by the route that God took for the redemption of humanity. The Resurrection, as well as the Incarnation, carries the body-life of humankind in a deep divine embrace. Redemption is not the promise of escape from the demands or appetites of the body. To confess that Jesus Christ arose from the grave bodily is to reiterate God's good feelings about his own creation of human beings as body-persons; to celebrate the Resurrection includes a celebration of human sexuality. God did not become man to show us how to get out of our body by means of spiritual exercises. He created a community of resurrection hope and invites us to bring our total sexuality into it. Christ's resurrection makes permanent God's union with the whole of humanity, and it thus affirms sexuality as part of our hope for ultimate happiness and freedom.

2. BODY-LIFE INTEGRATED

The gospel is a reaffirmation of the human body and therefore of human sexuality. But sexuality is not affirmed as an animal dynamic that surges solo in its own arena of hormones and genitalia. Human sexuality is not on a biological tributary running alongside but apart from the life of the soul. The gospel sets the vital springs of biological sexuality into the rapids of personal life. Sexual life is reintegrated into the personal life by the power of the Spirit. This is so because the body is wholly involved within the reality of the new creature in Christ. Sexuality cannot be left alone to seek its release or satisfaction apart from the new being of the person. The human body is the outer self made new in Christ along with the inner self.

Paul's attitude toward the body demonstrates that it, along with the soul, is integrated into the new being. In the passage where he recoils at the thought of a Christian buying sex in a bordello, he goes on to talk about the body's place in the life of the Christian: "The body . . . is for the Lord, and the Lord for the body" (I Cor. 6:13). That is, the Christian life embraces people wholly as body-persons. Our bodies are members of Christ (I Cor. 6:15). The Resurrection attests to the fact that not even death can break the union of sex and soul (I Cor. 6:14). All this comes down to a fact that we have stressed several times: we are body-persons, and we cannot sever our body-life from our personal life.

But this does not tell us *how* body-based sexuality is affected by Christian experience. Some have felt that Christian experience only offers new controls for sexuality: this means that Christianity's contribution to human sexuality is a new set of stricter rules. Others have added that Christian experience provides a new power to suppress sexuality, or a new motive to escape it. In both views, if the body is indeed for the Lord, it must be a body purged of sex. Sexual legalism is a reaction against those for whom the dichotomy of spirit and sexuality meant a flippant nonchalance about sexuality: in their view, since sexuality does not touch on the spirit, why not let it roam wild and free. What a person does with his genitals has no more bearing on his spiritual life than whether he drives a car or rides a bus. This is the kind of attitude that horrified Paul; for it led some Christian men to suppose that casual visits to the local bordello had no more bearing on their Christian selves than casual visits to a barbershop. Paul's response is to underscore again the nature of human beings as body-persons. You are, he says, bound to Christ as a body-person. You are, he repeats, a person whose body is destined for personal life in the kingdom of God. And what you do with your genitals you do as a person and, in particular, a person who is united bodily to Jesus Christ.

Thus it is true that the integration of our bodies into the life of Christ entails limits on our sexuality. But these are not to be construed as bridles on an untamable force from the abyss. The limitations on our sexuality are limitations on ourselves as persons. We do not fence in sexuality in order to release its hold on our persons; we fence in sexuality because it is part of the scenario we write with our personal lives.

This helps us understand Paul's otherwise odd remark about the seriousness of sinning against our bodies: "Every other sin which a man commits is outside the body; but the immoral man sins against his own body" (I Cor. 6:18). Now why does he say this? Oversimplifying other sins to make his point, he seems to say that sins like stealing, coveting, even lying, do not infringe deeply on a person's own selfhood. But sexuality involves our very selves. Sleeping with a prostitute commits a man's very person, even though he does not intend it to. The point is not that sexual acts are more serious than other acts because they are sensual. They are more serious because they are much more than merely sensual; they involve the deepest and most significant facets of our personhood. No Christian can make believe that sex with a whore is only a release of his bodily tension. Casual sex is a contradiction in terms.

3. FREEDOM IN CHRIST

"For freedom Christ has set us free" (Gal. 5:1). We must somehow let this speak to us as sexual persons. Everything in us must be set free in Christ. This has to be the pivot on which our sexual lives turn: "Where the Spirit of the Lord is, there is freedom" (II Cor. 3:17).

Sexual freedom is easily misunderstood. I will mention two misunderstandings. For some people sexual freedom has meant freedom *from* sexuality. They thought that if people were only led by the Spirit, as Paul said, they would be free from the "desires of the flesh" — which were then equated with sexual drives. And sexual drives were for them demonic urges from the abyss to lure the soul into damnation. So if they were really to be free in Christ, they would have to be liberated from their sexuality. But others have gone the opposite route, grasping freedom as escape from responsibility. Irresponsible sex takes the form of a license to get selfish physical satisfaction whenever, wherever, and from whomever it is available. This attitude has no better view of sexuality than the other. Repressed sexuality and casual sexuality both cut it off from the development of personal life; both reduce sexuality to a biological function. The difference is that one sees it as an enemy and the other sees it as a toy.

Being sexually free in Christ implies that our sexuality is a personal — not just a biological — reality. For Christian freedom is of the essence of a truly personal life. If sexuality is thus woven into the free life, sexuality must be very personal. Freedom always involves two poles: freedom from and freedom for. Freedom is a gift that liberates us from distortions and compulsions that hamper our development into genuine human beings. But liberation from compulsion and distortions is never an end in itself. We are always free to do, free to relate, free to serve, and free just to be, in Bonhoeffer's words, "a person for others." I will skim through some facets of both "freedom from" and "freedom for," and try to zero in on sexuality's place in both of them.

A. Freedom From

1) Freedom from Compulsion

Paul says we are liberated from what he calls "the law of sin and death" (Rom. 8:2). The "law" refers to a power beyond our control that drags us down to a destruction of our personal selfhood. We must take both components of Paul's statement very seriously. There is a law, a force, or a power that takes the form of compulsion; and the upshot of compulsion is the death of our free selves. Freedom from the power of sin and death can be translated into sexual terms very easily. Compulsion to use our physical sex drives to exploit other people is obedience to the law of sin and death. Freedom in Christ is freedom from impulses to exploit a sexual partner for one's own satisfaction; to possess another person as a thing depersonalizes both parties. Freedom from the law of sin and death also means freedom from compulsive domination by physical needs. Physical sex can dominate our sexual lives if we allow it to; and when it does, human sexuality has been lost to biological mastery. The life controlled and driven by biological sex is a life of personal emptiness, which is both "sin and death."

2) Freedom from Guilt

Paul says that there is "no condemnation for those who are in Christ Jesus" (Rom. 8:1). For too many this means no condem-

68

nation except in sexual matters. Why is it so much harder to accept grace in our sexual lives than in any other side of life? That it is can be attested by any counselor or therapist. Many Christians can accept forgiveness for almost anything but what they do with and feel about their genitals. Many people sing "Amazing Grace" under a cloud of undefined and unspecified guilt about sex. We cannot seem to emphasize it enough: to those who are in Christ there is absolutely no condemnation.

Freedom from guilt applies to real guilt as well as to false guilt. There is real guilt in sexual behavior, and freedom from condemnation does not eliminate concrete guilt for specific acts. It is one thing to say that I have sinned and been forgiven; it is another to say that I have not sinned. But there is no reason why sexual guilt needs to be suffered as though it alone were left out of divine forgiveness. The gospel comes to persons who have exploited other persons for sexual gratification and are in fact guilty. But for them, as for income tax evaders, there is no condemnation in Christ.

We are also liberated from false guilt. And here as nowhere else it is the truth that sets one free. Not long ago people felt shame because they fantasized, masturbated, or just felt sexy. Today they are likely to feel false guilt at inadequate sexual performances. At one time married people felt guilty about anything but eyeball-to-eyeball sexual relations; today they may feel a sense of guilt for being less than sexual virtuosi. Concerning false guilt also it must be said: there is now no condemnation, no judgment. And if there is no condemnation in Christ, there ought to be none in us directed against ourselves. Freedom in Christ means that he no longer condemns us for real guilt and that we need feel condemned for neither real nor false guilt. Christian prayer should include — along with "lead us not into temptation" — "deliver us from needless burdens of guilt."

3) *Freedom from Moral Tyranny*

Moral tyranny operates wherever the rules of a community are given a force equal to the will of God. When our groups — whether liberal or conservative — impose their rules on our consciences, they impose a moral tyranny that Christians cannot tolerate. For when the folkways of the group are translated as divine command and internalized as the will of God, they bind the conscience. And conscience is a holy citadel where only Christ has the right to command. Thus folkways that posture as divine rules are anti-Christ. It was against the substitution of religious mores for God's will that Paul issued his manifesto of Christian liberty: "For freedom Christ has set us free; stand fast therefore, and do not submit again to a yoke of slavery" (Gal. 5:1).

No tyranny is harder to break than the tyranny of sexual rules. Even when the rules themselves are ignored, the conscience may still be plagued by them. Where people submit their conscience to moral tyranny, they suffer pangs of condemning guilt as though they were assaulting the holy will of God himself. Who knows what inner shame people have suffered where no guilt was incurred? Who knows how often conscience has been pinned down and beaten by the rigid rules of sex-frightened groups? Unwritten rules about masturbation, sexual fantasies, and sensual pleasure in married sex have spurred people on to whip themselves with unearned guilt feelings. The gospel will never be experienced as good news for sexual beings until we learn to tell the difference between moral tyranny and divine law.

This does not mean that community customs never reflect God's will; however, it does mean that free Christians have the responsibility to discern when and if they do. Nor does it mean that free Christians will never conform to group rules; it does mean that when they do conform they will do so out of love for other persons, not out of moral obligation to the rules. Nor, of course, does it mean that there are no divine rules for sexual behavior; St. Paul, who fought for freedom harder than any Christian leader, brought up short those people who thought that because some things were permissible, all things were (cf. I Cor. 6:12-20).

We will have enough to say about moral law and sexual behavior later on. For now, let us say that Christians are free to be and do that which God does not prohibit, with love and concern for persons being the only strings attached. This means freedom from all moral tyranny.

4) Freedom from Illusion

One piece of good news is that Christ liberates us from the illusion that sexual technique is the route to personal joy. One gets the impression from some sex manuals available today that if we only liberate ourselves from sexual restraint and discover enough erogenous zones, we will make it to the full life. Or if we can only experience the ultimately volcanic orgasm, we will discover the joy of sex. If Christ liberated us from anything, it is from the illusion that sensual passion is enough to fill the vacuum of a personal life. Sexual athletes may well be emotionally and spiritually crippled persons. Physical climax is a deadening experience unless it contributes to, or at least is in tandem with, personal growth. Furthermore, sensual pleasure separated from personal growth is not true sexual enjoyment, for sexuality is too deeply rooted in personhood to be measured in orgasmic intensity.

I do not want to suggest that sexual technique is unimportant; it is very important. Couples can flounder in sexual frustration for lack of it. They can fail to achieve a loving sexual life simply because they do not know how to make love freely and effectively. Instead of being a means of sharing each other, sexual activity can be a block to sharing if it is bungled through inhibition or ignorance. Perhaps we should drop the word "technique" —

which is a rather mechanical notion — and talk again of the *art* of lovemaking. In any case, while bad technique or bad art can ruin love-sharing, good technique cannot create it.

This leads us to another illusion, the fixation on sex as though it were a real thing. Sex is really an abstraction. We talk about sex, write about sex, and teach our children about sex. But sex is nothing at all; only sexual persons are real. The ironic thing is that our obsession with an unreality called "sex" makes us prisoners of a myth. Perhaps this is why sex dominates so much of modern life: it is an abstraction promoted to the status of reality, and unreality turned into a myth tends to become a dominating force in life. And so we can seriously speak of our age as being demonized: we have come to worship at the shrine of a non-thing. Christ liberates from the illusion that the idol of sex has magical power that can make happy, fulfilled persons out of empty shells. He leads us into the freedom of persons who know that God is real, and that the real God wants us to be free from illusions about false gods.

B. Freedom For

Christian freedom is a liberation from depersonalizing powers that abort our growth into Christ-filled persons. To be free in Christ means to be a person-with-Christ; and to be a person-with-Christ is to be a person-for-others. What we want for others is for them to be free. Therefore, it is necessary to speak of freedom in terms of freedom for others as well as freedom within ourselves.

The person-with-Christ is the sexual person for others: sexuality in Christ is freed for loving service to another. It can transcend the urge for self-gratification without suspending it. But the law is: "He who seeks to save his life shall lose it." The search for sexual self-gratification is a dead end. Only when sexuality is integrated into the urge for communion with another will the whole self be sexually gratified. Sexual fulfillment, therefore, must be a lively, exciting, restless part of our desire to serve the other. And our service to others must be directed to the other's freedom as a person. This is true in the broad, nongenital sexual relations of men with women; the male-in-Christ will use his male role to further the freedom of the female-in-Christ. But it must be especially true of the ultimate sexual relationship — the sexual embrace of male and female. Sexual partners, as Paul said, will be "subject to one another" (Eph. 5:21), so that each can be free as a person. In short, we are free in Christ so that our sexual lives can be instruments of freedom.

C. Freedom In

Freedom is possible within an order limiting us extensively so that we can be the more free intensively. And a sexual life within its true environment is more free than promiscuous sex. Of course, sexual relations are not confined to marriage; but it is in the sphere of marriage that sexual relations can be truly free. For marriage provides the atmosphere of relaxed trust that the most intense sexual experience requires. Marriage accepted as a life-long partnership is the sphere in which two people can learn the secrets of self-giving in their impulsive abandon to sexual play. In marriage time is available for teaching one another how to be a rewarding sexual partner; here husband and wife can patiently teach each other the techniques of sexual pleasure. But more important, marriage provides the deep security needed for the abandonment that sexual freedom needs. We must get it into our heads that God sets sexual activity within an order not to dampen sex but to bring it to life and set it free.

4. SEX AND THE SECOND COMING

Paul's own grudging acceptance of sexuality must be understood in the light of his primary concern — Christian freedom. "I want you to be free from anxieties," he wrote in the chapter that has been labeled the antisex manifesto of the Christian religion (I Cor. 7). The advantage of a person free of the marriage bond was that he could serve the Lord unfettered in the little time that Paul thought was left. The problems of sexuality had to be resolved in terms of how men and women could most likely live the free life of service to Christ.

The Christians Paul was writing to were caught in an environment of open-ended sexual license: anything went in Corinth, and the result was sexual chaos. Some Christians thought they had found new grounds within their faith to endorse sexual license; after all, what a mere body does can hardly matter to the soul. But other Christians overreacted, thinking their faith militated against the body. They thought the best route was to avoid all sexual contact: Christians ought to stay unmarried. "It is good for a man not to touch a woman." (Presumably, it was equally good for a woman not to touch a man.) This is the sex-denying thought that Paul was responding to.

He answers in terms of freedom. The Christian response to sexual problems is for every man and woman to hang loose, neither frustrated by inner anxiety nor burdened by external obligations — free to please the Lord. Now the single person could be free from the outer anxieties of pleasing a spouse and of working at a marriage. In that sense, he agreed, it is good for a man not to touch a woman. All he concedes is that the single man who does not touch a woman can be free from the anxieties that a married man has "about worldly affairs, how to please his wife" (v. 33). On the other hand, being unmarried can leave a man frustrated with sexual desire or burning with temptation to fornicate. The tempted and frustrated single person is no more free than a harried husband or wife. Besides, he may actually yield to temptation. Not everyone is up to freedom in celibacy, and celibate lack of freedom is worse than the restrictions of marriage. Thus, for those who cannot be both celibate and free, marriage is the better solution. But in Paul's thinking, the best option was freedom from both unmarried frustration and married concerns. If one were not capable of the former, marriage was the safest, though not the ideal, option.

At this point Paul was not impressed by marriage as a partnership permanently built into human life by creation. In what he considered the last hour before Christ returned, freedom was more important than marriage. But marriage served to keep the spontaneous urges of the sexual drive in check; it was a fence for the libido. "*But because of the temptation to immorality, each man should have his own wife and each woman her own husband. . . . It is better to marry than to be aflame with passion*" (vv. 2, 9 — italics mine). Where the choice is between the furies of unrelieved passion on the one hand and marriage on the other, Paul is for marriage. But if one has the gift for it, celibacy with freedom from all sexual desire is even better, not for its own sake but for the sake of unhampered service to Christ.

Marriage, then, is a concession to weakness, not a created ideal. As Calvin puts it, Paul was not recommending marriage "with a view of alluring them to its delights as though he took pleasure in commending it." No, marriage for Paul is a "remedy for avoiding fornication." Earlier in the Bible, when life on earth was more promising, the writer of *Genesis* said that it was "not good for man to be alone." Paul argued that under the circumstances it *was* good for man to be alone. The disagreement is not blatant, but it is real. It was good for man to be alone provided he could truly be free in his aloneness. If he could not, it was right — though not ideal — for him to marry.

One credit not often enough granted Paul is his liberation of men and women from the obligation to marry. He did not root marriage in a creation order and thus seemed to reduce its importance; but at the same time he gave new freedom to the unmarried. The unmarried woman or man need not feel like an unwanted person; she or he has no intrinsic duty to be married and is free to decide to remain single. Callings and gifts differ in the sexual world as in all others. The main thing is to find the role in which each is free, free to serve the Lord as he or she is called.

5. CHRISTIAN LOVE AND SEXUAL LOVE

Where does Christian love touch down on our sexuality? How does the "love of God shed abroad in our hearts" get inside our experience of sexual love? Jesus' command was that we love one another as he loved us. But can we love sexually with the love of Christ? Do sexual love and Christian love run on parallel tracks that never intersect, or do they intermingle and become one?

I have been using the word "sexuality" all along to cover much more than genital desire. Human sexuality includes more than hormones, organs, and orgasms; it runs through the psychic and spiritual ranges of our lives. We experience our sexuality on the spiritual level as a yearning for another person. We want to reach out and stretch ourselves into the depths of another. We want to bring the other person into the orbit of our deepest selves. We want to probe into the mystery of the other. He is a mystery that tantalizes us and makes us want it to become the secret we share together. Only when we focus our longings on a single person and enter into radical life-union with that person do we have a complete sexual experience. The physical yearning is meshed with the spiritual, and this is the total experience of sexual love. To this yearning, longing, and seeking the Greeks gave the name *eros,* after their god of the same name. The following are a few characteristics of eros.

(1) Eros is born of need. We love sexually because we need to be completed by another person. The need is far more than a need for physical release; it is a need for intimate union with the whole self of another in order to complete ourselves. So eros is the movement within us toward the person whose life bears the promise of filling our need.

(2) Eros is selective. Not every person offers a promise of meeting our deep need. Eros is stimulated and wooed by those whose qualities offer that promise. Thus eros is discriminating: it separates the lovely from the unlovely, the attractive from the unattractive, the promising from the unpromising; and it responds to the promise that in one particular person we can be fulfilled.

(3) Eros is natural. No one needed a command from God to be pushed into love; no one needs an impulse from the Spirit of Christ to seek the promise of eros. Our need is woven into our created maleness and femaleness. We reach out to another because we are *created* to find our true selves in union with another, and because eros is a created good.

Now let us remind ourselves of some qualities of Christian love — by which I mean the love that brought God to earth to seek and save the lost. The gospel reveals a God who loves sinners, and in this lies the radical specialness of God's redemptive love. To the love of God for sinners the gospel gives the name *agape*.

(1) Agape is born not of need but of fullness; it is not a seeking but a giving love; it reaches out from strength to weakness. It does not reach out for fulfillment but to fill emptiness. It does not yearn to get what it needs, but empties itself to give what the other needs.

(2) Agape is indiscriminate. It does not select the good, the exciting, and the beautiful; it goes out to all — to the bad, the dull, and the ugly. It does not select only those who promise a satisfying response, but it moves to all, indifferent to their value, heedless of their worth, regardless of the promise they offer for fulfillment.

(3) Agape is supernatural. It does not rise from nature but transcends nature. It is human to seek what we need; it is divine to seek what others need. It is natural to want union with another to fill our own gaps; it is supernatural to want union with those who offer little and have offended much. It is supernatural for a holy God to love sinners.

Agape is so different in quality from human eros that some students (like Anders Nygren) have said the two have nothing in common, that they contradict each other and are irreconcilable. Others (like Paul Tillich) say that they are really the same thing, that they both arise from nature's urge for wholeness and are flip sides of one coin. Still others (like Thomas Aquinas) say that they complement one another, that God's love (*agape*), while unique, only makes human love (*eros*) better. I believe that they do complement one another. But how?

Let us begin by saying that Christian love does not substitute for sexual love; agape does not supplant eros. We need not go into the theological reasons for saying this, except to remind ourselves that the God of saving love is the same God who created us male and female. More to the point, allowing Christian love to crowd out sexual love would be the kiss of death for good sexual relations. Christian love is always given "in spite of" the shortcomings it sees in the loved one. A lover who lets the loved one know that the latter is loved wholly "in spite of" what he is will kill sexual love. In sexual love we seek and find what we need; but we also need to be needed. We must know we have something to give, that we are loved "because of" what we are. Furthermore, in sexual love we need a sense that our loved one is special; we need to select one from many. And we need a sense that we too are desired above any other. Agape is neighbor-love: it goes out to all people just because they are there and in need. But no wife or husband could abide being loved only with neighbor-love. And no sexual relation could remain whole and healthy on a love that is the same for everyone.

Agape cannot supplant eros even *in part*. Agape does not pre-empt the personal side of sexual love while leaving physical sex to eros. A loved one needs to be loved on all levels *because* of and not *in spite* of what he/she is. And a lover reaches out to the loved one on all levels — body, mind, and spirit — because of the promise he/she offers to the lover. To be attracted to a person's body in erotic desire, but to love him/her as a person only in sacrificial giving, would not redeem but only ruin sexual love. Eros must roam the ranges of sexual relations. When Paul tells husbands to love their wives with the agapic love of God (Eph. 5:26-27), he cannot mean for them to let agape crowd out eros. If he did, we would have to say that the apostle, though an expert on the saving love of God, was a fool on the sexual loves of men and women.

But if God's love cannot replace erotic love, it must somehow blend with it. We cannot divide life into love-tight compartments. We do not love on separate wavelengths, one for agape and the other for eros. We are just people who love. But different objects attract our love in different ways. For example, sometimes a person draws out of us only a giving love; he/she attracts a giving love because we see him/her only as a person who needs us. Sometimes, in the throes of restless need, we experience only a seeking love with a person who promises fulfillment for us. But more often we love with agape and eros flowing through each other. Christian and sexual love are blended, if not homogenized. The reason for this is simple: the people we love need us and we need them. They promise fulfillment to us and need fulfillment from us. We love another "because of" *and* "in spite of" what they are.

Christian love, then, can save sexual love by injecting itself inside it. It works from within in at least three ways: (1) agape enriches sexual love, (2) agape stabilizes sexual love, and (3) agape corrects sexual love. Let me try to explain what I mean by each of these.

(1) Agape enriches sexual love by its regard, concern, and

reverence for the loved one as a person. Reverence is the highest form of respect for the sheer personhood — the irreplaceable, mysterious self — of the other person. Agapic love pierces beneath all that eros finds attractive, and sometimes ugly, and finds the underlying self deeply hidden there. It respects that self by letting it be what it is, by willing its freedom and encouraging its hold on its own integrity. It steps back a pace so that the other can have freedom to be his/her own self. This, incidentally, is one reason why God's love is not *wholly* undiscriminating: it knows the difference between persons and things. It loves the sinner without regard for the sinner's loss of value; it has respect for the person hiding behind the face of the sinner. God does not love good dogs the way he loves sinful persons.

Agape also adds realism. Agape can look at the loved one and see him for the imperfect person he is. Though eros reaches out to the promise of fulfillment offered by the loved one, agape knows that the loved one cannot fulfill the promise wholly. For the loved one is not all that eros wants him to be. When agape is injected into the bloodstream of sexual love, it opens the eyes of the lovers to the impossibility of perfect satisfaction from eros. But as it opens their eyes to weakness in their loved ones, it also opens their eyes to their deepest worth — their mysterious, elusive personhood. Thus agape enriches sexual love with realistic respect.

(2) Agape stabilizes sexual love. Eros is doomed to instability. It flickers like a candle in the wind. Unchanging, undying erotic love is a myth. Sexual love is unstable because it depends on the other person's ability to deliver on the promise of fulfillment. At the physical level, sexual attraction rises and falls as the waves of desire grow and die; but even at the spiritual level, sexual love blossoms and fades as the loved one succeeds and fails to deliver on the promise of fulfillment. But agape is stable because it comes from a reservoir of love that is infinite and because it goes on loving "in spite of."

The strains on sexual love are sometimes very heavy. At the

physical base, impotence, frigidity, and any other dysfunction can strain sexual love to a breaking point. At the spiritual level, almost any personal blemish can dampen the flames of erotic passion. But agape, with its realism about perfect fulfillment and its regard for the person of the loved one, gives sexual love a stable base, a staying power for the cold winter of eros's temporary death.

But agape has one more secret power. It is able not only to keep a person in union with another when eros dies for a while, but also to help revive eros. There is a strange power in love: it can turn the loved one into what love desires. People tend to become what other people expect them to be. When the loved one knows he or she has been seen and desired, he tends to see within himself what the lover sees. When eros dies, the loved one may lose his loveliness because he knows his lover no longer sees him as lovely. That is when the power of agape can work its small miracle. For agape sees the person beneath the attractiveness that once promised fulfillment, and it reverences what it sees. And that reverence makes the loved one still feel valuable in his own eyes.

(3) Christian love corrects sexual love whenever it is distorted; and sexual love is very easily distorted. No matter how passionately it "worships" the loved one, its worship is largely for the sake of self-fulfillment. The egoism of sexual love is not evil; but sexual love, because of its biological roots, readily lapses into sheer libido or lust, cut off from desire for union with a person. Because of its yearning need, it can readily turn its needs into exploitation of the other. The progression from need to demand to the manipulation of another are the links in the chain of distortion within a fallen sexual world. Agape corrects the distortions of eros by its power of self-giving and concern, its regard for the person, and its desire to serve the good of the other. Agape blended with eros prevents one from turning need for fulfillment into exploitation; it can prevent us from slicing libido from the spirit. For agape keeps its focus on the person and moves outward — not to receive but to give.

81

Christian love, then, does not replace sexual love; it infuses it with a power that can revive it when dying, correct it when distorted, and enrich it even when it is alive and well. Agape gives will and backbone to the soft tissues of eros. Christian love, far from snuffing out passion, fuels the flames.

I have, of course, been talking about the *potential* of agape, not about the actual experiences of Christian lovers. Nor have I meant to say that non-Christian marriages are doomed to failure because they miss agape entirely. Christian people do not always live in the power of agape, and non-Christian people often share in a spillover of agapic power. Thus, very often Christian marriages fail for lack of agapic power, while non-Christian marriages manage. Besides, the failure of erotic love in some Christian marriages may be so complete that agape does not save it. Agape cannot create eros; it can only enrich, stabilize, and correct it. If there is no erotic love, agape cannot substitute for it — even when it is experienced in a powerful dosage. Failure of eros can hurt people so badly that they block the passage of agape into their lives. When this happens, they may have to get away from each other so that agape can come through to them again.

6. SUMMARY

The following is not a summary in the sense of a condensation of what has gone before. It is more like a distillation of thoughts that seem to be running through the material we have covered.

A. Sexuality Is Communion

What we experience in our own sexuality is a need for communion. It happens on the biological level as a need for pleasure and release; but the biological experience is only the substratum of the whole sexual urge. What we want in sexual satisfaction is to be close to somebody, to share the most intimate kind of exposure of ourselves, to give ourselves in spontaneous and uncontrolled trust to another. What we want, then, is the height and depth of personal communion and security.

B. Sexuality Is the Possibility of Pleasure

Our sexuality offers us fantastic pleasure. It is God's gift of creative grace that he made bodies so bent on having and giving pleasure. And no pleasure is so intense as the pleasure of erotic play. But sensuous and sensual pleasure alone cannot explain the unyielding urge; there is a need behind this ecstatic delight that not even the intensity of the pleasure accounts for. What is desired and needed is the sharing of the pleasure that comes with sharing of the self, the overcoming of individuality through communion. It is the intimacy of persons with persons, the giving of self and the taking of another, the communion that comes from uncontrolled, rapturous personal exposure in the embrace of another person. And this is the deepest pleasure our sexuality urges us to seek and to find.

The sheer physical pleasure is genuine and good. Bodies are made to be played with, just as bodies are made to play and to work. It is in play that communion is the closest: when sex becomes labor without humor and ecstasy, planned and controlled as a surgeon plans his strategy for an appendectomy, sex has lost its power to be spontaneous, and thus ecstatic, play. No one should ever be ashamed of sexual play, because communion is best at play. And communion is what God made us for.

C. Sexuality Is Transgenital

The sexual delusion of our time is that sexuality is only about orgasms. In this distortion, all sexual encounter between male and female is an anticipation of intercourse and orgasm. The evil that this distortion does is many-sided. One of the ills is that people who believe the heresy act it out; they assume that sexually tinged encounters must end in bed. This leads them either to a kind of fatalism about sexual intercourse or to a fear of any relationship that has sexual overtones. The fear, however, is not always a safety catch. Sometimes it leads well-meaning people to suppress the sexual dimension of a relationship, convince themselves it is all "platonic" or professional, only to have it break open on a physical level when their defenses are down.

Actually, whenever a man and a woman relate to each other as persons there is a sexual dimension in the relationship. The more deeply personal it is, the more sexually involved the relationship becomes. This does not mean that all personal encounters between a man and a woman are springboards to an embrace. But it does mean that there is present an undercurrent of varied and unpredictable sexual dynamics that we can call psychic sexuality. It adds an indefinable tinge of adventure and excitement, uncertainty and curiosity to the relationship. It colors the conversation with all sorts of brighter and lighter hues absent from the paler conversations between members of the same sex. The sexual dimensions of a totally "innocent" relationship provide the added adventure and mystery of personal relationships that a unisex society would sadly lack. Male and female relate to each other as sexually defined persons, and sexuality infiltrates and permeates every personal relationship. This we owe to our creation as male and female, not to some lecherous trait inherited from the fall of man. We should be conscious of it, accept it, and rejoice in it. The more we affirm it with thanks the less likely we are to be deluded by the fear that any sexually exciting relationship will lead to the bedroom.

D. Sexuality Is a Mystery

The mystery of our sexuality is one of the deep mysteries of our personhood. The mysteries in our own individual selves are compounded by the fact that we are never individuals alone, but are persons only in relationship. Even on the biological or physical level the mystery is present. Why is sensual sex so delightful? Why do people seek it so restlessly? Why is sexual pleasure so different from other pleasures of the body? Why is it at times so miserable and disappointing? Why does sexual intercourse at times leave one with an emotional hangover? We cannot get at the mystery and anxiety of sex in a quantitative measurement of sexual responses. Masters and Johnson report that there are some 34 erogenous zones on a female body, that spasms of male orgasm occur at .8 second intervals, that the female nipple expands 10 millimeters at the peak of sexual arousal. But knowing such trivia as this leaves the mystery of sex untouched. For the mystery of sex is the mystery of persons in encounter at all levels of sexuality.

It is, of course, possible to slice off genital pleasure from human sexuality. Where two people get together with no more involvement than genital excitement, they are really only masturbating in tandem. And they do not experience each other on the whole sexual spectrum. But where sexual encounter is a total and unreserved experience of two persons, a mystery is present that no one can fathom. There is an unveiling of the self to another; but even when one has disrobed his selfhood to another, the mystery of his self is still deep, intriguing, and unexplored. Hence, the sexual probing of one another never ends; it must be repeated over and over again. This is one reason why sexual intercourse, the radical exposure, is so intriguing and electric — and yet incomplete. One has to come back again, not just because the hormones have been recharged and need release, but because so much always remains untapped in the human encounter.

If we are sensitive to the mystery of sexuality, we also become aware of its possibilities. There is so much more than the ecstatic pleasure of orgasm with another person. What happens in sexual intercourse brings greatest pleasure when, in a moment of self-forgetfulness, an act of trust takes place: two persons fulfill their absorbing need to be totally within the physical and spiritual embrace of another person. This is why it is really not orgasm but the moment of penetration that is the critical point of one's first sexual experience. In a way, the pleasure of sex is the ultimate earthly pleasure because it is the most radical and complete fulfillment of humanity in communion. This is also, paradoxically, why sexual intercourse has an affinity with death: in death and sex a person must let go of himself and put himself in the hands and heart of another. In death one does it finally; in sex there is always another chance.

E. Sexuality Can Be Demonized

Persons are bigger than their sexuality. Persons are made for God: their center and their goal in life are rooted in the Being beyond the deep urges of sexuality, and they are created to seek and to find the kingdom of God and its righteousness. This is why the development of sexuality must take place within a galaxy of other dimensions of life, dimensions that involve them in multiple layers of social responsibility. This is also why the development of our own sexuality must happen within a profound awareness of the mystery and sacredness of other persons. But most of all, it must be subordinate to the final goal of life: to seek and find a personal relationship with God. Sexuality is not something on the fringes of our quest for meaning and relationship.

Sexuality is demonized when, instead of an urge to share one's self with another in the mysterious communion of persons, it is an urge to exploit, to abuse, and to destroy. But it is demonized on an even more sad and subtle level when people are driven by the illusion that physical sex — genital sex in itself — can *create* a communion between persons. Genital sex cannot take us out of our loneliness; it can only express a togetherness already found. And when one uses his genitals to escape the aloneness of his life, he is bound to be cast even deeper into the prison cell of loneliness.

Sexuality is demonized even further when, in the vacuum of despair, it is used not in hope of discovering communion but in hopelessness. Promiscuity can be a kind of hell into which those who have abandoned hope enter. Promiscuous people are sometimes only acting out their despair. The quick sexual encounter, repeated over and over, is not a grasp of hope but a private drama of hopelessness: "What the hell?" "Why not?" But the kernel of what sexuality could mean is still present, and the dim memory of it serves only to drive the actors more deeply into their despair.

F. Sexuality Affirmed by Grace

Grace is a word we give for God's free decision to accept sinners just as they are — for Christ's sake. To live by grace is to live by God's affirmation of ourselves just as we are, as he made us. Grace helps us to accept ourselves in our weakness and in our failures. Grace leads us to affirm what God himself affirms as the good he created. We have a hard time telling the difference between accepting ourselves *in spite* of our sin and accepting ourselves *because* of what we are. And our sexuality gives us the greatest trouble in this respect: the sensual urgings, the restless desire arising from some dark depth within us — are these reasons for having to accept ourselves "in spite of" what we are? Or does grace reveal that these are good, and that we are accepted by God even because of them?

Grace does not destroy nature; neither does it despise what

God has made. Creation and grace are together in God's mind. Redemption restores what we have corrupted and distorted, including what we have distorted in our sexuality. But redemption does not turn us from sexuality; it illuminates the goodness of it. There are two biblical texts that we must, by all means, keep together when we wonder about grace and sexuality:

> So God created man in his own image . . . male and female he created them. (Gen. 1:27)

> And the Word became flesh and dwelt among us. . . . He was in the world, and the world was made through him. . . . (John 1:14, 10)

The same Lord who became man for our salvation, and who brought grace and truth to the world, was the Lord through whom our sexuality was called into being. For grace is of him "through whom all things were made," including the reality of being male and female.

The discovery of grace is the discovery of creation's goodness as well as the discovery of sin's badness. It is the discovery that we can accept ourselves as sexual because our sexuality is one of the most exciting sides of the life God created for us. Somehow, though we don't know how, our sexuality will be enhanced and glorified in God's perfect heavenly kingdom just because it is the gift of God on earth. Christians should be those who sing the praises of sexuality most loudly. For it is they who are in on the secret: Jesus Christ has "broken down the dividing wall of hostility" (Eph. 2:14), including hostility between the sexes, so that our sexuality can again — in freedom — be a mysteriously wonderful drive toward personal communion. Grace heals the distortions of sexuality so that the power of sexuality can come into its own.

PART TWO

SEX AND
SINGLE PEOPLE

CHAPTER FIVE

Sexual Intercourse

We move now from the wide ranges of human sexuality to the specifics of sexual behavior. In this chapter we will focus on the morality of sexual intercourse for single people. Mainstream Christian morality reserves sexual intercourse for married people. Our purpose is to ask why. Why have Christians, until recently, set this one act apart and declared it off limits for single people? What is morally unique about coitus? To put it frankly, why does Christian morality put such a special premium on the insertion of a male sex organ into a female vagina? Is there more than the merely physical in this physical encounter? If so, what is the special significance? The question has a double focus: first, what is special about coitus that it should be available for married people only? Second, what is special about marriage that it alone qualifies people for coitus?

One thing is statistically clear: whether or not God says no to sexual intercourse for single people, more and more single people are saying yes to it. For one thing, the majority of American young people have adopted a new standard for the rightness of sexual intercourse: the standard is sincere affection. Ira Reiss's surveys have shown that most single people, especially college

91

students, believe that coitus is right provided the two people have strong affection for each other (*Premarital Sexual Standards in America,* 1964). For another, surveys have shown that premarital sexual intercourse has been a common, if hidden, fact of American life for a long time. We were taken aback in 1953 when Alfred C. Kinsey's research revealed that 33 percent of women under twenty-five had had premarital sexual intercourse (Kinsey's 1948 research had revealed this to be true of 80 percent of 25-year-old men). As a matter of fact, other surveys had shown roughly the same percentage for two decades before that. But the 1975 results of a *Redbook* magazine questionnaire (to which 100,000 women replied) reveal that 90 percent of the women under twenty-five who responded said they had engaged in premarital sexual intercourse. Now, every one of these women may have made a moral error. But the point we must note is that the mainline Christian code — continence outside of marriage — does not control the behavior of most American single people.

We have no sure way of knowing how many Christian people have accepted sincere affection as the moral standard for sexual intercourse. (Although the *Redbook* survey reports that 75 percent of the under-25 age group who said they were strongly religious have engaged in premarital sex, these are not necessarily reliable statistics on the percentages of Christian single people who in fact have.) Not all of them have. And one can assume that in villages and towns, and on conservative Christian campuses all over the country, there are still many single people who believe and live by the traditional Christian norm. But I also know from experience that more and more Christian people are no longer sure of *why* they do; and no one can be sure of how long they will.

My purpose is to probe the biblical rationale for the veto of sexual intercourse for single people; it is not to trace the cultural reasons for its wholesale neglect. But we should be aware that sexual morals do not change simply because a generation ignores traditional standards. It is obvious that biblical sexual morality has lost its hold on most people; but this is as true of business and political ethics as it is of sexual ethics. That secular society is not salted with Pauline morality in a conspicuous manner on any level is a truism. But Christian people are often at loose ends sexually just as non-Christians are. Even if they still follow the rules, they often do not know why. And there are reasons other than sheer moral apostasy that help account for changes in the sexual behavior of single people.

The most obvious fact about today's single people with respect to sex is that they have grown up in a sexually supercharged era. They have been bombarded by sexual stimuli as no other generation has. The single most powerful sexual stimulant in existence is the film; its seductive lure is almost overwhelming. It is difficult to imagine that any young person who watches today's films regularly could ever again feel — let alone think — about sexual intercourse in the same way that his parents did. There are also the best-selling novels, whose pages tremble with sexual agony and ecstasy. As for commercials, no one has yet gauged the influence of the use of sex symbols to sell almost everything the public consumes. So when we judge their morals, we must recall that young people did not ask to be reared in a sexually exploitative age; they were shoved into a culture that we older people created or at least tolerated.

One of the effects of media exploitation is that sexual intercourse has lost its moral mystique. The moment of penetration no longer has the aura of an earth-shaking moral event in a person's life. Technique has replaced morality as the crucial question to ask about sex: technique in gaining the opportunity and technique in performance. Not long ago I was asked to take part in a discussion of sex at a secular campus. In fact, the inclusion of the moral aspect on the program was an afterthought. Just before my turn to speak, a professor of psychology exquisitely explained to a crowd of college students how to achieve the "atomic orgasm." Morality came on as a tail-ender. This, I think, is not atypical of what college professors think students want to hear.

Actually, in my judgment, most single people place physical sex itself in some category beneath their highest priority. While it is true that sexual intercourse has lost its moral specialness, it is also true that sexual intercourse is not single people's most basic need. What takes top priority is the hunger for close personal relationships. It is, I think, a mistake to suppose that single people are all lustfully rushing to get into bed with someone. What is happening is that single people are infected with a terrible loneliness, and the filling of that closeness gap is uppermost in their needs and desires.

Of course, the need for closeness is part of the sexual package. Our very sexuality, while biologically based, is experienced as a reaching out for closeness with another person. Our culture brings physical sex into the picture very early as a means of finding and experiencing closeness. Other forms of personal relationships have become very hard to create; the neighborhoods, schools, and churches that formerly provided considerable opportunity for personal relationships fail us now. So the burden falls on the family, where closeness seems to be ready-made. But the family has to provide more than it can give; in fact, it is breaking under the burden of too much demand on it. As a result, alienation from parents is par for the course among adolescents as they move out toward independence. Indeed, engaging in sexual intercourse is often as much an act of resentment and rebellion against parents as it is a groping for closeness with someone else. It is hard to know in a given instance which is foremost.

In any case, what single people are looking for — whether they are adolescent or far beyond — is not, in the first place, a chance to get their hormones satisfied. They are looking for a chance to experience the reality of a personal, trusting, and complete communion. And they have been led to think that sexual intercourse has the most intense promise of providing it. So the result is a deep desire for personal intimacy together with the loss of moral urgency about the sex act. Behind all this personal restlessness, of course, lie the technical advantages of our time. The traditional fears that seemed to support morality have been erased by technological innovations. Conception, infection, and detection have been — it is supposed — done in respectively by the pill, the antibiotic, and the Chevy van. These do not explain the loss of moral inhibition; but they make the search for closeness that much safer and easier.

I do not pretend that this brief sketch explains the whole cultural push toward sexual intercourse among single people. But it is worth thinking about for this reason: we must remember that in moral issues the character of the actor is as important as the character of the act. My interest in this chapter is the moral ingredients of the act. I think we must examine the bases for our moral judgments concerning the act of sexual intercourse if we are going to get anywhere near a Christian evaluation of what is happening. Meanwhile, I think we also need to keep a compassionate eye open to the reasons single people violate what Christians have long believed to be a divinely given moral norm.

In the face of all this, we must get to the bottom of true Christian sexual morality. If the Christian standard is based on fear, it can be replaced by lessons in biology. If it is a pious trick to make sexual life more difficult for young people merely to teach them the virtue of self-discipline, the trick will not work. Sexual morality has to stand up on its own; the value of self-discipline can no longer support it. If Christian morality is a legalistic set of rules devised by antisexual ascetics, it could not possibly persuade Christian people in our sex-affirming time. If the prohibition of sexual intercourse for the unmarried is born of obsession with sheer genital virginity — as though mere penetration separated the chaste from the unchaste forever — it will be a weak moral stance indeed. And, finally, if Christian morality has no compassionate sense of the differences between people and their motives for engaging in sexual intercourse — no feel at all for the moral difference between sheer physical exploitation and a genuine act of love, or between two irresponsible people acting in a fit of passion and two mature adults acting in tender responsibility toward each other — it will seem insensitive and indifferent to the facts of real life. I say these things in order to stress the importance of our question: what is the real reason Christian morality segregates the unmarried from the married and qualifies only the married for the climax of sexual experience?

Two other things need to be said, if only to avoid misunderstanding about why we are focusing on the specific question of sexual intercourse. First, I am aware that, while intercourse is the cutting edge of sexual morality for the unmarried, it is by no means the only question. Premarital sexual behavior covers everything sexual from the first time an infant discovers pleasure in handling his genitals. It includes the morality of erotic fantasies, of masturbation, of petting, and all the fascinating things one can find in a glossary of sexual terms. Second, unmarried people have only one thing in common: they do not have a spouse. Beyond that they range from bewildered high school sophomores to prim widows playing shuffleboard in a Florida retirement village. All of them have sexual needs and sexual problems, and each of them experiences sexual relationships in his own way. These and many other variables remind us that we cannot separate the question of sexual intercourse from human differences. Still, sexual intercourse is the cutting edge of all the other questions, and it is the one question on which Christian morality has traditionally had a single clear answer.

My plan is to work up gradually to the New Testament morality of sexual intercourse. We will look at three moral attitudes first, each of them bringing us a step closer to the Christian moral stance. Then we will ask what the New Testament, Paul in particular, has to tell us about sexual intercourse and its moral quality.

1. THE MORALITY OF CAUTION

Any reasonable single person trying to make a rational decision about his sexual activity will "count the cost." The first thing they may ask is: "Am I likely to get hurt?" Sexual intercourse has some risk along with certain possible rewards for unmarried people, and the cautious person will weigh the risks. The question of "getting hurt" has two parts: (1) how seriously can I get hurt, and (2) how great is the risk of getting hurt? If the odds are not good and the possible hurt pretty serious, the cautious person may decide to wait until marriage, when the risk will be mostly eliminated.

The hurts that sexual intercourse could cause unmarried people are obvious enough. Getting pregnant, even in a permissive society, is a painful experience for an unmarried woman. Once pregnant, she has no way of escaping a painful decision: she can abort the fetus, she can give the baby up for adoption, or she can rear the child herself. Or, of course, she can get married — but this may not be an option for her. The route of abortion has been paved by liberalized laws. But no matter how easy it may be to get, and no matter what her intellectual view of abortion may be, she is likely to find out afterward that it is a devastating experience for herself, especially if she is sensitive to the value of human life. Adoption is another route. Every child given up for adoption may be God's gift to some adoptive parents. This is a compensation. But giving up children nourished to birth inside their own bodies is something few young women can do without deep pain. Keeping the baby and rearing it may be easier than it used to be. Many communities no longer lash the unwed mother with their silent judgment: this may be only because the community does not care, but it still makes life easier for the mother. But rearing the baby alone is still heavy with problems for the unmarried mother in the most tolerant society. Some may have a chance at marriage; but marriage forced on two people is an invitation to pain. In short, pregnancy can cause considerable hurt.

While pregnancy still hurts, the risk of it is not threatening to many unmarried people. However, any notion that the risk has been eliminated is careless thinking. The contraceptive pill has cut the chances, but it has not removed the possibility. Unwanted children, both in marriage and out of it, testify that no birth control device known up to this point is failproof. And, of course, there is the risk of that accidental time when precautions were neglected. As a matter of fact, the majority of young people having intercourse for the first time do not use any preventive means at all. Many young women refuse to take precautions because they do not want to think of themselves as planning for intercourse; it must happen only as they are swept into it in a romantic frenzy. Still, all things considered, the risk of pregnancy may have become small enough so that the cautious person may decide it is worth taking.

The threat of disease is a real one, especially for the promiscuous person. Antibiotics, once heralded as a sure cure, have stimulated virus strains more potent than ever. And venereal disease is currently in a virtual epidemic stage. Still, for prudent and selective people the odds seem comfortably against infection.

The risk of threatening an eventual marriage by premarital sex is hard to calculate. A deeply disappointing sexual experience before marriage could, one supposes, condition a person against happy sex in marriage. But, of course, unmarried people considering intercourse do not plan on having a bad experience. Guilt feelings about a premarital experience can inhibit one's freedom of self-giving in marriage sex: for example, a woman's inability to experience orgasm in marriage is sometimes traceable to guilt about premarital sex. And promiscuity before marriage could possibly make extramarital sex easier to fall into should marriage sex be unrewarding. But all these threats depend too much on how individual people feel; they are not useful as blanket judgments. The question of threat to marriage has to be answered in terms of the individuals involved.

Jane, who believes religiously that sexual intercourse before marriage is a sin, runs a fairly strong chance of making marriage harder for herself by premarital intercourse, especially if she has sex with someone besides the man she marries. But Joan, who was reared in a moral no-man's-land, may not risk marriage happiness at all by having premarital sex, though she may risk it for much deeper reasons. All in all, the argument that sexual intercourse by unmarried people threatens their future marriage is a flimsy one; too much depends on the moral attitudes of the persons involved. This implies, of course, that one does not have to be one hundred percent moral to have a happy marriage, though it may help.

The morality of caution leaves us with no clear-cut decision. Christian morality cannot support a blanket veto of sexual intercourse for unmarried people on this basis. It all depends on how the risks are calculated in each person's situation. The morality of caution will lead prudent people to ask with whom, why, and when they are having intercourse. But it is not enough to tell them that they ought not do it. Following the morality of caution alone, sexual morality comes down to this: if you are reasonably sure you won't get hurt, go ahead.

The point to notice is that the morality of caution is concerned only with possible hurt to the person involved. It does not bother with questions about the kind of act sexual intercourse is; it does not ask whether unmarried people are morally qualified for it on the basis of either their relationship or the nature of the act. I do not suppose that many people, in their best moments, will decide on the basis of caution alone. But wherever it is snipped away from other considerations, it works on the assumption that sexual intercourse as such has no more *moral* significance than a gentle kiss.

2. THE MORALITY OF CONCERN

Here we move beyond caution to a personal concern about the risk of causing hurt to others. The morality of caution asks: am I likely to get hurt? The morality of concern asks: am I likely to hurt someone else? The calculations of both moralities are roughly the same. The difference is that here concern is directed toward the other person. The crucial questions here will be how far one's concern reaches and how sensitive one is to the kinds of hurt he could cause. It may be that the concerned person will interpret the risks differently than the merely cautious person will.

For instance, a girl may be willing to take the risk of pregnancy as far as she is concerned. But if she considers the hurt that pregnancy may involve for the unwanted child, she may weigh the odds quite differently: the risk of pregnancy will be the same, but the possible hurt to others may count against having intercourse more heavily than if its pleasure is matched only against possible hurt to herself. If she gets pregnant, the girl may decide to abort or give the child up for adoption. The fetus has no choice. Here she is dealing with a potential person's right to exist. If she gives the child up for adoption, she is determining that the child will not be reared by its natural parents. And if she decides to keep the child, she may be forcing a situation of permanent disadvantage on another human being. This may sound as though only the woman is making the decision; but the same considerations must go into the thinking of her partner. By his act he may be risking severe disadvantages for another human being — or at least a potential human being — and giving that human being no choice in the matter. The unmarried couple may be able to opt for the risk; but the unwanted offspring is not given a chance to weigh the odds.

But again, the risk may seem small enough to take for the sophisticated person. And for some couples there is always a back-up emergency plan — marriage. But here again the element of concern is brought in: are the people involved reasonably sure that they won't hurt each other by getting married? The person with concern will ask the question and seek advice in answering it: but only he or she can give the answer for himself.

No person who makes decisions out of concern for others will run much risk of infecting another person with venereal disease. And a person who is truly concerned will be least likely to be a threat: he would not likely be a person who goes in for casual bed-hopping. The risk is not great for two people who are serious about sexual intercourse as an expression of deeply involved affection because the probability of promiscuity is not great. At any rate, the morality of concern would tell a person to be very careful, but it would probably not tell him to abstain from sexual intercourse entirely.

Personal concern looks a lot deeper than the risk of getting someone pregnant or spreading a disease. A concerned person will wonder how sexual intercourse will affect his partner as a whole person, because each person's sexual experiences are a major theme in the symphony he is creating with his life. No one can take sex out at night and put it away until he wants to play with it again. What we do with sex shapes what we are; it is woven into the plot of a drama we are writing about ourselves. The person with whom we have sexual relations cannot let his sexual passions dance on stage, take a curtain call, and go back to some backstage corner to let the rest of the play go on. So a concerned person will ask how a sexual experience can fit into the total life — the whole future — of that other person. Where will it fit in his memories? How will it be digested in his conscience? What will it do to his attitude toward himself? How will it help create the symphony that he can make of his life? The morality of concern reaches out into the tender tissues of the other person's whole life; and it refuses to endorse any act that will stunt that person's movement into a creative, self-esteeming, and freely conscious life.

However, it also goes beyond the other person. It asks about the people around them — their friends, their families, and their community. A single, discreet, and very secret affair may not bring down the moral walls of Jericho. But a Christian person of concern will think beyond his own affair: he must universalize his action and ask what the effects would be if unmarried people generally followed his example.

Much depends, naturally, on the kind of sex he is thinking about. If he is thinking about casual sex, on the assumption that all two people need for good sex is to like each other, we have one set of problems. If he is thinking about sleeping only with the person he is planning to marry, we have another. If he is thinking of casual sex, he will have to ask about the burdens on society created by a considerable number of unwanted children, a formidable increase in venereal disease, and a general devaluation of sexual intercourse as an expression of committed love. But if he is thinking only of sex between two responsible people who are profoundly in love — though not legally married — the question is limited to what the effect on public morals would be if everyone in *his* position felt free to have sexual intercourse. He might respond by saying that if it *were* moral for him, it would be moral for others. Thus public morality would not be damaged if everyone did it; habits and customs might change, and moral *opinions* would change, but morality itself would be unscathed. And he would be right — on this basis.

Concern for the other person and his community sets the question within the perimeter of Christian love. It comes within the single blanket law that all of our decisions are to be made in responsible love. In the terms of this morality, sexual intercourse is morally neutral, and the question of its rightness or wrongness is answered only in relation to its consequences for other people. If the risk of harmful consequences is small enough, single people are free to go ahead. The morality of concern forces people to judge according to circumstances; for

102

example, the answer to the question whether two mature retirees should refrain from sexual intercourse may be very different from that concerning two youngsters on a sexual high. Acting only out of loving concern, one puts aside the possibility that there may be something special about sexual intercourse that disqualifies everyone but married persons. It demands only that each person weigh the risks carefully and then make a responsible decision for his particular case.

3. THE MORALITY OF
PERSONAL RELATIONSHIPS

Two things set off the morality of personal relationships from the first two: first, its focus is on how intercourse will affect the *relationship* between the two persons; second, its concern is more positive. The clinching question is whether sexual intercourse will strengthen and deepen the relationship. If it can be a creative factor in the relationship, it is good — provided, of course, neither person gets hurt individually. Behind this way of deciding the right and wrong of intercourse lies a whole new understanding of human beings as persons-in-relationship. The view is that the individual comes into his own in relationship: the "I" is a truly human "I" only as it exists in an "I-You" relationship. The tender spot in human morality, then, is always at the point of personal contact with another. And this is why the effect sexual intercourse has on the relationship is the pivotal question.

The relationship can be creatively supported only when two people have regard for each other as ends to be served rather than as means to be used. When two people use each other in sexual intercourse, they hurt the relationship and corrupt the sexual act. They twist the relationship into a functional association. One has a functional relationship with a person whenever he concentrates on getting a service from him. What one wants

103

from a plumber is to have his leaky faucet fixed; what he wants from a dentist is to have his toothache cured; what one may want from a sexual partner is to have his ego served or his sex drive satiated. In these cases one is after a functional association. But what someone wants in a personal relationship is to let the other person thrive as a person, to give him the regard and respect he merits as a friend, and to be privileged to grow into a relationship in which they will both desire no more from each other than mutual concern and enjoyment. In short, he wants the other person to be something along *with* him rather than merely to do something *for* him.

Now in most cases, two people in love treat each other in both functional and personal ways. There is constant tension between expecting one's friend to deliver the pleasures of friendship and respecting him only for what he is. In sexual love, the functional side often *tends* to shove the personal side into the background. The sex drive is so intense that it becomes a temptation to manipulate and even exploit the other person. To the extent that the functional is predominant in our sex lives, we treat the other person as a means and thus dehumanize him. When this happens, sexual intercourse is immoral, not because it is sexual intercourse between two unmarried people but because it distorts and destroys a personal relationship.

Sexual intercourse can deepen and enrich a personal relationship only when it takes place within the reality of a personal relationship. This means that the preliminary questions two unmarried people must ask each other are: Do we already have a genuinely personal relationship that can be deepened and enriched? Do we have deep personal regard for each other? Do we treat each other now in integrity? Do we say no to any temptation to use each other? Did we accept each other as friends before sexual intercourse entered our heads? The possibility that sexual intercourse might be good for them travels with the answers to these preliminary considerations. Then they have to ask the clinching question: will sexual intercourse deepen and enrich or will it threaten and distort our relationship?

But how can they possibly know what it will do? First of all, each person has to examine himself. He or she will have to probe his/her own feelings and ask personal questions about them: Is he being exploitative? Is he pressing the other person to do something he/she may not want to do? Is he minimizing the other person's freedom and dignity? But these questions are about negative factors that could hurt the relationship. How does he know that sexual intercourse will actually strengthen the relationship? This exposes the Achilles' heel of the morality of personal relationships.

Furthermore, how can this standard be applied? How can two unmarried people know ahead of time whether sexual intercourse will enrich their relationship? They could probably try it and find out. But that would summarily throw the moral question out of court. And perhaps this is the only way out for the morality of personal relationships. At best, the decision has to be made on very uncertain personal insights: the people involved can only guess beforehand what will happen to their relationship after they have gotten out of bed. They can probe their readiness with all honesty and still not know for sure how they will feel toward each other afterward.

If we were talking about two people's date for dinner or a concert, almost any risk might be worth taking. But sexual intercourse opens trapdoors to the inner cells of our conscience, and legions of little angels (or demons) can fly out to haunt us. There is such abandon, such explosive self-giving, such personal exposure that few people can feel the same toward each other afterward. And if one thinks he is ready, he cannot be sure the other person is. The problem is not just that one of the two will feel sour toward the other; the problem is that one of the partners may unleash feelings of need for the other that he/she had no inkling existed. He/she may thus be catapulted into a commitment that the other is not ready to take. And so the relationship can be injured by one person's making demands on it that the other is not ready for. And the person who is least committed is likely to withdraw inwardly from a relationship that demands more than he can give.

If we could somehow segregate people according to maturity, and if only people over fifty used the morality of personal relationships, we might have a workable standard. If, in addition to this, the decision were made with moral assistance from a community of friends and family, it might be a usable norm. And if the decision were made in the cool of the day, it would at least be manageable. But unmarried people moving toward sexual intercourse include many people whose experience in durable and creative relationships is almost nil. A decision concerning sex is often made alone in the passions of the night, when every untested lust may seem like the promptings of pure love. Perhaps there is a moral elite who could responsibly use a moral guideline with as many loose ends as this one; but there is no way of knowing for sure who they are.

So we are back where we started. Each of the three moralities for sexual intercourse focuses on factors outside the act itself. None of them assumes that sexual intercourse has a built-in factor that in itself would disqualify unmarried people for it. But Christian morality has traditionally believed that there is such a factor. For it has maintained that, even if nobody gets hurt and even if a personal relationship could be enriched by it, it is wrong for all but married people. It has taught that there is more to sexual intercourse than meets the eye — or excites the genitals. Sexual intercourse takes place within a context of what persons really are, how they are expected to fulfill their lives in sexual love, and how they are to live together in a community that is bigger than their private relationships. We now go on to ask about this special ingredient of sexual intercourse, for it stands behind the traditional Christian negative to unmarried people.

4. THE MORALITY OF LAW

New Testament morality on this point is a morality of law. Some things were morally indifferent; Paul insisted on this. For some things there was no law except the law of love; and love flourished in freedom. But when people, as in Corinth, applied Christian freedom to sex, Paul put up fences. One of the fences was marriage. He made no distinctions between casual sex, sex between engaged couples, or sex between mature widowed people. The no was unqualified. The question is: Why?

Before getting into Paul's sexual morality, we must concede that the Old Testament gives him shaky support. Female virginity had a high premium; but male virginity was not all that important. And female virginity was demanded not so much for virginity's sake as for social reasons: the family line had to be guarded at all costs. And the male in particular had a right to be absolutely certain that his children were his own. The society had no place in it for the unmarried woman, no place except the brothel. So the rules said that if a woman had sexual intercourse before marriage, then tried to fake virginity with her bridegroom and was exposed by failure to produce a bloodied sheet, she would be executed forthwith (Deut. 22:13-21). However, this was probably not likely to happen. If a man slept with a virgin who was not betrothed, he was obligated to pay a dowry to her father and marry her (Deut. 22:28-29). And the prospects for an unmarried girl who had lost her virginity were so bad that no woman was likely to keep quiet about the affair. She would at least tell her father, who, threatened with loss of dowry, would put the fear of God into a reneging sex partner. A man was in real trouble, however, if he slept with a virgin betrothed to another man; he was in trouble with her fiancé and with her father, for it was especially their rights that he had abused. He would be stoned to death; and if their act was discovered in the city, the woman would also be stoned — on the assumption that she failed to cry

107

for help (Deut. 22:23-27). But if a man slept with a prostitute, nothing was said because nothing was lost. Casual sex between young people, however, was probably nonexistent. Once a boy slept with a girl, he was expected to marry her; and the girl was not likely to be noble about it and let him off the hook.

The Old Testament as a whole did not read the seventh commandment as a no to sexual intercourse between unmarried people. The morality of sexual intercourse did not rest with the character of the act as much as with its possible consequences. What was wrong was for a man's rights to be violated. Unmarried sex violated the command against stealing as clearly as it did the command against adultery.

The New Testament looks at the question from a very different standpoint. It has a blanket word for sexual immorality: *porneia,* translated as fornication in the older versions and as immorality in the newer. Fornication includes more than sexual intercourse between people who are not married. It does refer to breaking one's oath of fidelity to a husband or wife (Matt. 5:32; 19:9); but it could include a lot of other practices, like homosexual relations. And Paul makes clear that it also means sexual intercourse for unmarried people. In I Corinthians 7 he concedes that to be both unmarried and a virgin is, under the circumstances, the best life. But "because of the temptation to immorality, each man should have his own wife and each woman her own husband" (I Cor. 7:2). Better to marry, he said, than to be ravished with unfulfilled desires. So he must have meant that "immorality" included sexual intercourse outside marriage. And if unmarried sexual intercourse was wrong, it was a serious wrong; it ought not even be talked about (Eph. 5:3). God's will is that we abstain from fornication, not giving way to "the passion of lust like heathen who do not know God" (I Thess. 4:6). Fornication is sin; intercourse by unmarried people is fornication; therefore, intercourse by unmarried people is sin.

We must now ask the crucial question about Paul's blanket

rule. What is there about sexual intercourse that makes it morally improper for unmarried people? Surely not every instance of coitus by unmarried people is simply a surrender to lust "like the heathen." And if it is not in lust, and it hurts no one, why is it wrong? Did Paul assume that it would always be in lust or would always be harmful? And if some unmarried people's sex was not lustful, would it then be morally proper? Divine law, though often expressed in negative rules, is rooted in a positive insight. The law against adultery, for example, reflects a positive view of marriage and fidelity. And this view of marriage rests on an insight that God created men and women to live out their closest personal relationship in a permanent, exclusive union. We may suppose that behind Paul's vigorous attack on fornication is a positive view of sexual intercourse.

Sexual intercourse involves two people in a life-union; it is a life-uniting act. This is the insight that explains Paul's fervent comment on a member of Christ's body sleeping with a prostitute (I Cor. 6:12-20): "Do you not know that he who joins himself to a prostitute *becomes one body* with her?" (v. 16 — italics mine). Of course, Paul is horrified that a prostitute is involved: a Christian man is a moral clown in a brothel. But the character of the woman involved is not his basic point. Paul would just as likely have said: "Do you not know that he who joins himself to the prim housewife next door becomes one body with her?" And the incongruity would have been the same. Paul bases his remark on the statement in Genesis 2 that "the two shall become one." And he sees sexual intercourse as an act that signifies and seeks the intrinsic unity — the unbreakable, total, personal unity that we call marriage.

It does not matter what the two people have in mind. The whore sells her body with an unwritten understanding that nothing personal will be involved in the deal. She sells the service of a quick genital massage — nothing more. The buyer gets his sexual needs satisfied without having anything personally difficult to deal with afterward. He pays his dues, and they are done with each other. But none of this affects Paul's point. The *reality* of the act, unfelt and unnoticed by them, is this: it unites them — body and *soul* — to each other. It unites them in that strange, impossible to pinpoint sense of "one flesh." There is no such thing as casual sex, no matter how casual people are about it. The Christian assaults reality in his night out at the brothel. He uses a woman and puts her back in a closet where she can be forgotten; but the reality is that he has put away a person with whom he has done something that was meant to inseparably join them. This is what is at stake for Paul in the question of sexual intercourse between unmarried people.

And now we can see clearly why Paul thought sexual intercourse by unmarried people was wrong. It is wrong because it violates the inner reality of the act; it is wrong because unmarried people thereby engage in a life-uniting act without a life-uniting intent. Whenever two people copulate without a commitment to life-union, they commit fornication.

Thus Paul's reason for saying no to sexual intercourse for the unmarried goes a crucial step beyond all the common practical reasons. We can suppose that Paul would appreciate anyone's reluctance to risk getting hurt; we can be sure he would see a Christian impulse in a person's concern for the other person; and we may assume that he would endorse the notion that sexual intercourse ought to promote the personal relationship between the two partners. But his absolute no to sexual intercourse for unmarried people is rooted in his conviction that it is a contradiction of reality. Intercourse signs and seals — and maybe even delivers — a life-union; and life-union means marriage.

There is no question that Paul's view runs against the grain of common sense and experience. However, common sense tells one that a piece of bread and a glass of wine do not carry an invisible load of supernatural grace. But does that prove that they do not? Some people have no sense of God's urgent presence in them and the world around them. Does that prove he is not there? Many people have sex without any sense of being personally united with their partners. One can do anything with genital sex: one can sell it, give it away, or loan it out for an evening. Paul knew that people all over the world violated his sense of reality with no trace of awareness that they were doing so. Grossly insensitive people see no beauty where beauty throbs. Grim people are insensitive to humor where the situation is enormously funny. In the same way, people high on sexual technique, jaded by sexual indulgence, and scornful of sexual rules may be dead to what Paul is saying. But this is neither here nor there. The question is whether Paul sees reality as it is.

We have been trying to uncover the positive insight that lies beneath Paul's stern negative to intercourse for unmarried people. He sees something very special about sexual intercourse; it goes beyond the earth-shaking orgasm and even the conscious self-sharing of two personalities. It cannot be captured on a frame of pornographic film or even in an erotic masterpiece. It cannot be tested with electrodes attached to erogenous zones of the body. It can only, in the last analysis, be believed. But whether believed or not, it is the special reality on which Paul's uncompromised law of abstention rests. Coitus is an act that typifies and — in a way not made rationally clear — seals a life-union between two people.

Can we make sense of it? Are there any signals from our own experience that carry resonances of Paul's message? One thing that we feel today about ourselves is in tune with Paul's point: our sense of the oneness of soul and body. We sense that our bodies are not mere baggage carried around by souls, to be discarded when we die. When our stomachs hurt, we hurt; when our bodies are seasick, we are seasick; what we do with our bodies, we do with our selves. Christians may sometimes piously talk as though souls were some sort of air bubble inside their bodies; but ordinarily they act as though their bodies are their

111

very selves. Our bodies *are* us — the outside of us, but still us. This reflects Paul's view: a person's body was his outer self and his soul was his inner self — not another self. When a body is the temple of the Holy Spirit, the person is a temple (I Cor. 6:19); when a person glorifies God in his body, he is glorifying God as a person (I Cor. 6:20); when a person gives his body to be burned, he gives himself to the flames (I Cor. 13:3); when a Christian yields his body as an offered service to God, he yields himself (Rom. 12:1). And when two bodies are united in sex, two *persons* are united. The body is the person, the outside person that touches the world around him.

This is why genital sex is always, in some way, personal sex. Some Corinthian Christians supposed that sex was merely a body function: it did not matter what the Christian did with it. Paul said that it mattered a lot. It matters because the body is the person, though not the whole of him. Nobody can really do what the prostitute and her customer try: nobody can go to bed with someone and leave his soul parked outside. This is why a lot more is involved in sexual intercourse than the celebrated "joys of sex." The persons are involved because, creatively or destructively, the soul is in the act. The physical side of sexual intercourse is a sign of what ought to happen on the inside. It is the final physical intimacy. Two bodies are never closer: penetration has the mystique of union, and the orgasmic finale is the exploding climax of one person's abandonment to another, the most fierce and yet most sensitive experience of trust. Afterward, the two people seldom feel the same way toward each other again. They may love each other as never before; they may resent each other; they may only feel comfortable with each other. But after intercourse, the relationship is somehow not what it was before.

If normal experience with intercourse at least hints at Paul's sense of the mystery in it, we can grasp something of the deeper reason for the traditional Christian veto of it for unmarried people. Sexual intercourse is meant to be a personal life-uniting act;

therefore, it is proper only for those who intend a life-union together. A life-union is marriage. Therefore, marriage alone qualifies people for sexual intercourse. The demand for continence is not a killjoy rule plastered on the abundant life by antisexual saints. It is respect for reality as Christians understand it. The moral law fits the inner reality of sex.

We must now come to terms with two caricatures. The first is drawn by stretching Paul's point to its legalistic limits; the second is a stupid moral point drawn from what Paul does not say. The first has to do with the life-union Paul talks about; the second has to do with sexual intimacy that comes technically short of intercourse. I will deal with them in that order.

First, the matter of life-union: what sort of life-union is this? Is it created infallibly by any act of sexual intercourse? Does it exist no matter what the couple's intention is? Are people, then, married in some mysterious sense the moment a vagina is penetrated? Are they married "in God's sight" simply and automatically once they have had "carnal commerce" with each other? Let us consider a simple example. Two young people have intercourse in frenzied passion after their high-school prom; are they forever married? And if they go their separate ways to different colleges or jobs, and each marries another person, are they committing adultery by their marriages? Consider another example: a young man sleeps with a prostitute during wartime. Later he comes home and marries his old girlfriend. If he becomes a Christian, is he obligated to leave his wife and go back to live with the prostitute he once slept with because he actually created a life-union with her? Chances are, if he tried, the prostitute would have him thrown off the premises.

We could, I suppose, twist Paul's feel for the mystery of sex into a magical power that locks two people forever into a closed circle called marriage. But this would be a stupid literalism. The fact is that Paul does not tell us *how* two people become "one flesh" by having sexual intercourse. His style is to keep us dangling

113

by the invisible thread of mystery. He often does that with other things — the sacrament, for example. What he tells us is that sexual intercourse has more going on in it than meets the eye. The physical intimacy, the abandonment in trust, the unique closeness — all these things hint at and become a sign of a deep personal union sealed between the two people by physical union. Exactly *how* remains a mystery. But it is enough to tell us that where the deep personal union is lacking, the sign and seal of it ought to be left alone.

Biblical sense says that what happens after the high-school prom in "innocent madness" is deeply inappropriate. What happens in a big-city brothel does not match its inner meaning. The youngsters lunged into a life-uniting act with no life-uniting intentions. They ought not to have done it because it is appropriate only for those who intend what the act signifies. But sexual intercourse does not unite two people forever in an absolute, literal sense, unless they *intend* to be united. Paul was not dealing with automat sex; it is not as though one inserts an organ and out comes a marriage. He was establishing this truth about sexual intercourse: it is a sensual act with spiritual implications, a physical act with an inner meaning. Therefore, the act is immoral unless it is joined by an intention to accept what the inner meaning signifies.

The second caricature is that of technical chastity. Paul seems to say that sexual intercourse is the one sexual act with special moral meaning. Does this mean that everything else is permitted? Someone might take Paul's view and argue this way: intercourse is the great divider; once a vagina is penetrated, chastity is lost. So as long as two people keep their genitals apart, they are in the safety zone of chastity. Two people may pet to orgasm every night and be on the safe side of chastity. Meanwhile, two single people may fall lovingly or compulsively into the fatal insertion and be exiled forever into the shadowy land of unchastity. But this line of simple legalism only shows how easy it is to distort a valid moral insight.

We could misunderstand Paul's point in another way: since sexual intercourse is a life-uniting act, we could suppose that all sexual intercourse within marriage automatically unites two people in an experience of living partnership. But this is obviously not true, and it is not what Paul is talking about. We know that sexual intercourse can be a horribly frustrating experience within marriage. In actual experience, it can divide and alienate people; more, it can be exploitative and dehumanizing. So, instead of being life-uniting, it can be life-alienating. The moral insight that sexual intercourse is an act that signifies life-union does not mean that it always expresses or creates life-union in our actual experience. It is something like taking the sacrament: the fact that the sacrament *signifies* the grace of God does not mean that people who take the sacrament automatically *receive* the grace of God. But it is still true that only people who intend to receive God's grace ought to take the sacrament of grace. In short, Paul is not telling us that everything short of sexual intercourse is morally right. And he is certainly not telling us that all sexual intercourse in marriage is morally right and spiritually creative. He is focusing on a single point: sexual intercourse is morally appropriate only for people who intend the life-union that the act signifies.

Given the caricatures that people have drawn from Paul's moral insight, it is no wonder that many Christians are telling us that we need a new definition of chastity. A common argument heard today is that people are chaste if they are sincere, respectful, and responsible in their sexual relationships. In this way of thinking, the act itself is empty of moral meaning. It seems to me that this is wrong. Sexual intercourse can be morally inappropriate even if the people involved are sincere. They could be both sincere and wrong. It may be much better to be sincere in having improper sexual relations than to be insincere. But it is, in the New Testament sense, better to be both sincere and morally right.

Caricatures, however, do indicate the presence of real problems. We will go on to discuss some of them. We will talk about how a life-uniting partnership is related to weddings: does a couple have to "get married" to qualify for life-union? Then we will talk about petting. After that, we will go on to ask about the many problems people face in the real life of marriage and sex.

CHAPTER SIX

Why Get Married?

We asked who was qualified for sexual intercourse. The New Testament answered: people who intend to live together. We asked why. And Paul answered: sexual intercourse signifies and seals a personal life-union. We asked how. But Paul did not answer; he simply told us that when two people copulate they do something that binds them in a life-partnership, which the Hebrews called being "one flesh." Still, while the relationship between sexual intercourse and life-partnership was not precise, it was definite enough to tell us that only people who intend the latter were qualified for the former. Therefore, liking each other a lot is not enough. Enriching a personal relationship is not enough. Only a commitment to a total and permanent partnership is enough to qualify people for sexual intercourse.

For most of us, a commitment to a life-partnership is the same as "getting married." But some of our sons and daughters do not make the same connection, "Living together" has become almost as common on larger campuses and in larger cities as "going steady" used to be. While it is still rare in smaller towns and on the smaller — especially Christian — campuses, cohabitation has become an accepted life-style wherever college-age people live away from home and where the college does not act as substitute parent. And even if it has not been digested into the style of the Christian campus, it is likely to become a minority practice there eventually.

The ground rules of cohabitation without a license vary. They run the gamut from going very steady to quasi-marriage. I will skip the more subtle nuances and point to two options. First, the young people who live together — full-time or most of the time — without pretending anything permanent like marriage have a partnership that is much more than "going steady"; but they do not mean it even as a prelude to marriage or a trial marriage. They are not trying marriage on "for size." The deal is completely open-ended: either partner can call it quits whenever he or she wishes. They make love but do not make commitments. They want more than casual sex but less than life-union. What they want lies somewhere between the uncertainties and anxieties of "going steady" and the certainty and commitment of marriage.

Before pronouncing moral judgment on this kind of life-style, we should at least try to understand. Compassion should be the cutting edge of moral judgment and understanding the cutting edge of compassion. In the first place, cohabitation is probably not a lustful lunge for sex on a regular basis. In our culture, young people can find enough sex without having to live together to get it. What, then, is the main motive? I think the main motive is a need for personal closeness, for a relaxed, open, dependable, and deep relationship with another person. Sexual intercourse is an ingredient of such a relationship, and its importance varies from couple to couple. But what is valued highest is the satisfaction of being close to someone who cares but who does not make heavy demands.

If this is true, "living together" is the young person's answer to one of the deep needs of our time. We have all come to put a high value on personal relationships, mainly because they are so hard to come by. Our neighborhoods do not give them to us;

institutions are large and impersonal; friendships are *ad hoc,* depending on the temporary associations of business and sports; deep and personal ties are not even easily formed in church. We live in what Vance Packard rightly called a "nation of strangers." So we value most consciously what we miss and need most deeply. We are all hungry for closeness.

Young people feel the need most urgently. They grew up in neighborhoods of indifference; they have often felt alienated from their parents' styles and values; and they are lonely within the huge information factories called universities. Besides, they have become skeptical about the institutional side of life in general — and of marriage in particular. So why not find closeness in the simplest way, a sexual partnership without the bondage of commitment or bother of legality? Furthermore, there is a certain logic that moves from a romantic definition of marriage to "living together" for the time being. If love is what marriage is all about, why can one not have all the experience of love without a marriage license? Besides, since love is what marriage is all about, partners choose each other without interference from their families. Marriage, once a merger of families, is now only a merger or two people. And if this is true, why should not the two people choose their own style of arranging their lives together? Whether or not the argument is sound, it has a convincing ring to young people.

Finally, sexual intercourse has lost its moral mystique. Young people, as far as I can tell, tend to think of it on a more practical basis. It may still be a special form of getting close, but it is not necessarily an expression of a total life-union. Paul's belief that sexual intercourse makes two people "one flesh" simply does not get through to the average secular young person. The traditional rules are ignored; but, more importantly, the biblical insight into the moral meaning of sexual intercourse is not even a conscious option.

From the Christian viewpoint, "living together" on an open-ended basis is morally inappropriate. There is no way to justify it on New Testament grounds. This is not simply a matter of breaking traditional rules: it is a matter of one's view of the deeper meaning of sexual intercourse. It may also have important practical hazards that raise many questions. Does it lock people into a deep relationship they are not ready for? Does it trigger emotional attachments on the part of one of the partners that the other does not share? What, in short, is the potential for emotional pain? Does open-ended cohabitation condition young people to shun all permanent commitments? And will it, for that reason, make their eventual marriage a shaky partnership from the beginning? Does it tend to reduce sexual intercourse to a mere expression of close friendship and so open the doors to extramarital affairs after marriage? Does it delude young people with the fantasy that living together for a while is really like marriage? Does it keep them in the illusion that deep and total partnership can come without struggle, agony, disappointment, and a constantly renewed will to create a true partnership? Does it, in short, give a cheap answer to the problem of loneliness and alienation? I suspect it does. I suspect that open-ended cohabitation is an infantile solution because it grabs the goodies of life without the long-term responsibilities of life. It achieves instant closeness but avoids the tensions and conflicts that are built into a life-partnership that is achieved only by a love that is willing to struggle.

We can put all these questions to the young people involved, but in the long run they will not be powerful considerations. For every red flag we wave they can find a green light to counter it. Cohabitation, they will argue, can be a useful preparation for marriage. It may make young people less impulsive and more rational in choosing their mates for marriage. And, within the new sexual ethos, having sexual intercourse does not trigger either strong commitment or deep guilt. In the end, the practical factors leave parents and young people in a standoff. The only question that can finally decide the issue *morally* is: what is the real meaning of sexual intercourse?

We have been talking about people who live together without commitment to each other. But many people live together with a kind of commitment, and yet do not want to get married. These are the people this chapter is mainly about. They intend something like marriage, and they do not see why a piece of legal paper filed in a clerk's office could make their partnership more meaningful, moral, or real than it is. The fact that they do not get married seems to betray some reservation in their commitment; but they feel as though it is a real one nonetheless. We could say that their commitment is more intensive than extensive. Their sharing is total, even though they do not want it institutionally extended into permanent wedlock. It is as permanent as they can make it at this point, but they are unwilling to gamble on a long-term future. Their relationship is not stable enough to fit the label of a "common law" marriage, but it is as stable as they can manage for now.

Why couples do not want to get married varies with each partnership, so we can speak only in generalities. But often these people are simply not able, within themselves, to make a permanent commitment. Their entire lives have been spent in uncertainty about the future; how can they now sincerely place their persons-in-relationship on the line for as long as they live? They also hate to contemplate the hassle of divorce should they not be able to keep their partnership going. If it should come to that, they want to be able to split without the nasty complications of a legal divorce. Some of them are no doubt reacting to the hypocrisies of many modern marriages. Serial monogamy, they see, is not prevented by legal or even church weddings. Some of them grew up in homes where the hallowed ceremony was an initiation into a cold war. Furthermore, a cynicism about all social institutions filters through their rejection of a wedding. These and many other motives lie behind their reluctance to gather the clan for a festive and solemn wedding ceremony.

Against this background, we must ask about the morality of

121

weddings as the right way to begin a sexual partnership. And in so doing we must admit that weddings are often moral farces. Moreover, the institution planted in a wedding is often an empty shell that binds two people together for a while in a hell of hostility or a purgatory of boredom. People do get married with little more than a hope that things will work out; and a hope is not a commitment to life together as long as that "life shall last." We must also understand that there is no moral law that tells us how we must begin a marriage. Marriages are not created only by the words of a justice of the peace or a preacher. Myriads of splendid marriages have begun without anything like what we would recognize as a wedding in our culture. And who knows how many weddings have legalized sham marriages? The Bible has a lot to say about marriage, but it has little or nothing to say about how marriages must begin. There is a theology of marriage, but there is no divine morality of weddings. Marriage is an invention of God; weddings are inventions of cultures. So when we ask why young people ought to "get married," we are asking why they should submit to a cultural custom that changes as culture changes. We will have to put up with an answer that carries less weight than divine law.

It seems to me that the correct moral category to use in fluid situations like this is responsibility. We do not always have clear moral law at our disposal, but persons are always called to responsibility. The responsible person is one who responds with human sensitivity and intelligence to each situation as it calls for a decision. We respond when we take stock of the claims our life-situation makes on us, interpret their meanings, and calculate the effects of our action. We respond when we use our wills and determine to be accountable for our actions. In the absence of rules, being responsible means giving the most fitting and helpful response we can to the situation that calls for a decision. A responsible Christian person will respond to his total situation as he sees it in the light of what Christ wills for him and for all who are affected by his actions. Thus, when he asks, "Why should we get married?" the responsible person will give his response in the light of such factors within his situation as the claims the state has on him, the claims of the church, the claims of his family, the claims of his partner, and the claims his own future has on him.

Moreover, our response has to be given in our own situation. A young man and woman living in the simpler days of Abraham would only have had to look tenderly into each other's eyes, go off by themselves to a tent, and make love; they then would be married. In that culture a network of clearly understood — though unwritten — laws, plus the supporting closeness of the clan or tribe, would have held them together in a marriage more stable than are most marriages in a society crisscrossed by detailed legal codes. But today's young people cannot be responsible within Abraham's culture; they can be responsible only within their own. If the same couple were alone on a desert island, they could be truly married without intervention of church or state. But most couples are not alone on an island. They can be responsible only in their situation: they have to do the humanly and Christianly responsible thing in the advanced and legally complex culture of the twentieth century. How it is done in Samoa settles nothing for a couple in Chicago.

There are two essential issues that involve every couple in "getting married": (a) whether they will play the game according to the rules set by the state; and (b) whether the couple is willing to begin a new relationship with a public declaration.

First, a responsible person will at least give a serious answer to the claims that legalities have on him. Civil laws concerning marriage require records to be kept because married life in modern societies becomes complicated. There will be children, property and income taxes, deaths, burials, inheritances, possibly divorces, and many other contingencies. Future decisions may need to rely on records of the people involved. Legal marriages are for the benefit of married people: they protect people against

123

disease, involvement in bigamy, and other technical disasters. Legal marriage also safeguards the privacy and intimacy of the couple; it guards the rights of the married couple against unwanted intrusions by third parties into their partnership. And it guards the rights of children if one partner should die or leave.

Furthermore, the laws of the state are there as an expression of an ordered community. If everyone made marriage only a matter of the heart, only a private thing in the hearts and minds of two people, a large dimension of society would be in a chaotic mess, and many people would suffer unfairly. The so-called institution of marriage supports, not diminishes, the possibilities of personally creative marriages. So the claims of the state are really protective claims. The occasional "unmarried" partnership is feasible only in a society where most people do honor the claims of society. Therefore, the question of whether to get married must be decided in response to the claims of the community on married couples.

Second, there is the matter of a public declaration. A responsible person will want his "style" to fit the real ingredients of his action. If it is true that when two people marry they are creating a new social entity within the community, their style ought to fit this fact. In the Christian view, a marriage is not only a private affair between two people who happen to live under the same roof. These two people form a new unit, and as a unit their relationship to the community is not the same as it was when they acted simply as individuals. They can pretend to be two individuals who happen to live together; but in fact they have formed a new social entity and have accepted a new status in the community as a married partnership. If this is true, what is the responsible way of initiating the partnership? Getting married is a couple's way of affirming publicly that they intend to accept the responsibilities of what their marriage makes of them: a new social unit within a society of such social units.

For Christian couples there is another community involved:

the fellowship of Christian people in the church. The church is a supporting and disciplining community. When Christian people get married and thus form a social unit within that community, it is their way of openly accepting the community's support and discipline. When a couple gets married "in the sight of God and these witnesses," they are saying that they seek and accept the prayers, the counsel, and the discipline of the church. And the responsible couple will by their wedding declare in community that they are prepared to live as a partnership within the supportive fellowship.

Finally, there is one more thing about marriage that asks for a wedding: it is the human need for festivity. Human life seems to need moments set apart for celebration and partying. We mark birthdays, anniversaries, graduations, births, and any other special event in our lives by breaking the routine of our life-style with a party. A person needs something to make toasts to; so does the community. And weddings are festivals celebrating the beginning of a new adventure. God's blessing on a marriage, given at a wedding, is really an act of celebration: the wedding affirms that a good and important thing is taking place. But again, there is no specific morality involved. Responsible moral decisions are made when persons size up the total picture and respond to it in a fitting way. Weddings are the public beginning of a new enterprise, which is at its heart the original private enterprise. Like all private enterprises, it needs the support and the restraint of a community. Weddings are not society's trick to keep young people in line with custom; they are this society's method of receiving a new enterprise of love into its midst.

There is no moral law that demands a wedding, and it is perverse to identify real marriage with weddings. A marriage without a wedding is not per se an immoral arrangement, and a marriage begun with a wedding is not per se a moral one. But being Christian and human implies a calling for persons to give an accountable response to all the dimensions of their actions. In view of that calling, a cogent case can be made that getting married is more responsible than living together without bothering with the institution.

CREATIVE COMPASSION

Compassion is an experience of suffering with someone else's condition. It is neither pity nor moral softness; it is a feeling-understanding from inside the other person's situation. Compassion gives us an insight into the unique situation and individual character of people who do something that moral principle tells us is improper. Creative compassion provides the sensitivity with which the moral law can be introduced into concrete situations — not to soften the law, but to apply it realistically. Without compassion we always miss some vital component of the personal situation; without moral law we tend to substitute sentimental tolerance for reasonable judgment. Thus, anyone who invokes moral law ought to wield it with compassion. But creative compassion offers the possibility of dealing with real people whose acts may be wrong in the light of moral law.

As we noted earlier, the line between chastity and unchastity cannot be drawn through the technical fact of intercourse. People who manage to avoid genital contact can be unchaste; and unmarried people who do have sexual intercourse do it for different reasons, with differing motives, and under differing circumstances. Compassion sees these differences. Law allows us to see only the dimensions of the act; compassion helps us see the moral quality of the person. Compassion does not change the moral principle; nor does it let us predict in advance those unusual situations when unmarried people might properly engage in intercourse. Creative compassion is guided by moral law, but it evaluates people's acts with an understanding born of "suffering with" them and provides the power for dealing with them redemptively.

A girl may grow up with an ugly complexion, hating the face she sees in the mirror. Her chances for dating in high school have been almost nil, and she is sure that no man will ever give her a chance for love. Her face, she fears, deprives her of the love her heart yearns to receive and return. She gradually learns to hate herself. Then a man comes along who is able to look beyond her face into her character. Their friendship grows into affection, and they discover that each needs the other. But neither is able, for deep psychic reasons, to make a commitment without reservations. So they move into an apartment to share each other's uncommitted love; each is free to leave whenever he/she wishes. Neither deceives the other with phony hopes of marriage, but each respects the other as a person and wants his/her growth and good. But they are not married, and so they are disqualified for sexual intercourse.

Two retired people, widowed or divorced, discover their lives enriched and renewed by their love for one another. In their maturity they are capable of a personal relationship in quiet yet exciting depth. They receive from each other a shared intimacy of sexual union that is profoundly loving; yet they cannot be married. In the first place, they could not survive on the reduced social security benefits they would receive if they married. In addition, they fear that a marriage may be hotly disapproved of by their children. And there may be any number of other obstacles to a legal marriage. So they merely visit each other regularly, including overnight visits, and commit themselves to each other on this basis.

Creative compassion evaluates these people in the light of their situation, refusing to put them in the same category of unchastity as casual bed-hoppers. Compassion does not undo the law, but it helps us see that moral law is broken differently by different people. Moral law judges that these two young people and two elderly people are doing a morally inappropriate thing; but compassion recognizes that they are doing it for purposes and with motives that put them in a category different from that of people who use sexual intercourse to dominate or exploit other persons.

Creative compassion tempers one's judgment of persons. Moreover, it moves in to create as good a situation *personally* as can be made of what — under moral law — is a bad situation *morally*. It may also lead a couple to see that marriage is an option for them in spite of their fears. It may bring them into a community where loving people are ready to support them in the weak commitment they are able to make to each other. It may sensitize them to the deep hurt each could cause the other should they call the relationship off. In short, creative compassion leads a couple into a situation where obedience to moral law seems feasible and, where that fails, supports them in the best possible relationship under the circumstances.

Compassion is not the soft underbelly of morality; it is morality's creative edge. It is creative because it judges people in the light of their circumstances and because it tries to help them to change their circumstances. And it is creative because it stays with people in understanding and love even when they reject the good guidance of moral law. Finally, compassionate judgment is not for third parties alone: the people involved must be helped to judge themselves in the light of their situation. An unmarried person who feels guilt for having broken the law must be as compassionate toward himself as others ought to be toward him. Self-judgment must also be tempered with the insights of compassion, lest one destroy himself with incrimination. What this really means is that the Christian moral lawbreaker can accept both the forgiving grace and compassionate understanding of God.

CHAPTER SEVEN

Responsible Petting

The great American game of petting deserves a fair appraisal. But it is very difficult to precisely define. Petting includes a wide range of body exploration, and every adolescent group has its own definitions of light and heavy petting. Petting falls somewhere between an affectionate embrace and sexual intercourse, and it can be roughly identified as fondling one another's sexually excitable areas. Maybe our problem with the morals of petting stems from our preoccupation with coitus as the one sexual act with serious consequences. The result is that petting is judged only in terms of the likelihood that the two people will lose control and plunge mindlessly into sexual intercourse. In this view, petting is only a prelude to penetration, a one-way street to intercourse — with no natural exits. They began on the route leading only to intercourse; and since sexual intercourse is wrong for unmarried people, petting is wrong as well. Thus, petting is extended foreplay; it is appropriate only for those who intend to have intercourse and therefore appropriate only for those who intend marriage. Morally speaking, those who pet to any extent and manage to stop before coitus are guilty in the same way that a burglar is guilty if he breaks into a house but runs before he can grab any loot.

129

Out of practical concern, those who look at petting this way usually call attention to the frustrations experienced by young people who engage in heavy petting. Petting brings on neuroses because of its abortion of a natural process. It brings on guilt feelings because young people themselves sense that they are involved in an activity that aims at — even if it does not arrive at — sexual intercourse. For practical reasons, then, as well as for moral ones, young people are counseled against petting.

There is some common sense about this view. After all, sexual foreplay between married people is a form of petting. But we don't call it petting. What is the difference between foreplay and petting? Perhaps the difference is nicely defined in the terms themselves: foreplay is a tender preparation for coitus, while petting is a tender exploration of one another by two people who do not intend coitus. The only question is whether sexual relations can tolerate intimate physical touching as an end in itself. Let me go on, rather bluntly, to give my opinion.

Petting can be a delicately tuned means of mutual discovery. It need not be a cheap way of having the thrills of starting out toward intercourse without the derring-do to finish it. Petting can be an end in itself. It can be a process in which two people explore each other's feelings with no intention of having intercourse. Communication can take place that conveys personal closeness and sharing, with flexible but recognizable limits. It demands, of course, a sophisticated sense of appropriateness if it is not going to trap the players in a fondling game that goes beyond the implicit limits of their relationship. And this, in turn, calls for education of young people in responsible relationships. Thus petting is a tender route that *could* lead to coitus, but need not intend to go that far. It has many natural exits, each of which is marked by invisible signs that indicate the place to stop, according to the amount of involvement that the two players have with each other as persons. It is not a cataract that carries partners over the falls of passion unless they halt the plunge and suffer the lesser fits of frustration. It is an adventure in personal understanding and intimacy that calls for control and discipline.

This view of petting conveys a truth about sexual relationships that Christian people sometimes neglect: sexual relationships have many meanings, and they are not all preludes to intercourse. Sexual relationships can include psychic awareness of being male and female in personal communication with each other — with coitus not even on the horizon. They may also include flirtation, petting, mutual masturbation, and finally coitus; but they need not include any of these. And it is untrue to the many nuances within sexual relationships to suppose that they all are defined simply by how many steps they are from their natural end in sexual intercourse. There is room within the large variety of sexual relationships for mutual exploration, mutual expression of affection, and mutual discovery of the meaning and depth of the sexual relationship, each as an end in itself at the time. Petting may be a way of sharing some intimacy without the ultimate intimacy being in consideration. In this sense, it can be an avenue leading to a clearer understanding of the depth of the relationship between two people; it can be a way to discover their real attitudes toward each other and toward themselves.

Petting is a halfway house between shunning all physical sexual expressions on the one hand, and rushing swiftly toward sexual intercourse on the other. But petting can also be a one-tenth or nine-tenths of the way house. The deeper and closer to commitment the personal relationship is, the more heavy the petting properly becomes. But a halfway house can be the terminal for some people. The practical worry of those who see petting as a one-way street to coitus is a real one, which we must recognize if we are to be realistic. Young people do not always have the ability to evaluate the quality and depth of their relationship, and often do not hear the signals that tell them when their terminal point of appropriate intimacy has been reached. It must be remembered also that petting is not a cool and calculated personal exploration; it involves increasingly heated passions that all too quickly send self-control into limbo. Therefore, the practical question is how petting partners can possibly be self-critical and sensitive enough while their passions are aroused to recognize and respect their proper terminal point when they reach it.

Realistic awareness of what happens to young people in the actual process of petting is what prompts moralists to judge petting as part of a package with coitus. This is why they apply the morality of law to petting. But, of course, this will not really do: the dynamics of sexual relations are too complex to put them all into the category of natural passages to the bedroom. Moreover, it is psychologically important to insist that sexual relationships are not all stages en route to penetration. The importance comes to this: the more we believe that all sexual relationships have only the bed as their terminus, the more people involved in sexual relationships will act on this premise. Their action will take one of several forms. Out of fear, they may needlessly cheat themselves of the creative experience in personal growth that can come from innocent sexual relationships; or they may indulge in innocent sexual relationships with a burden of false guilt; or they may get into the habit of experiencing every bit of sexually interesting communication as an inner push toward sexual promiscuity, and then act accordingly.

But if a simple moral prohibition of petting does not match the complexities of noncoital relationships, what is the answer? The Christian answer is the development, through spiritual exercises (prayer, conversation, counsel, self-criticism, openness to the Spirit), of personal responsibility. Personal responsibility does not in itself guarantee that anyone will know what is right and wrong at any given point. But being responsible means that a person is sensitized to give a genuinely personal response to the situation and its requirements. A personal response is an answer that comes from sensitive awareness of all the ingredients involved in a person's actions; it is a decision to act in a way that is appropriate to the personal and social dimensions of the situation. Some situations do not have a simple yes or no built into them; they must be accepted as a summons to personal responsibility. The moral issue of petting is one of these.

But if we avoid legalism, we should also avoid naiveté. Petting is a risky game, and the players are not always responsible players. There is a wave of sheer lust and exploitation lurking in anyone — young or old — even though they mean to be responsible as Christians. It is as easy to exploit another person in petting as it is in intercourse; perhaps nowhere is a person more vulnerable than in petting. Hopes can be falsely aroused, and disguised lust can be mistaken for affection. A person's intense desire for love can translate the other person's lust into a message of genuine love. The rule of responsibility in petting requires a perception that not every person has, once his passions are aroused. The lonely youngster, the child who receives no affection at home, the person who has little self-esteem — this is the person for whom petting is a gamble. He/she needs to be wanted so badly that he/she is ready to interpret anybody's desire for conquest as a gesture of affection. In order to rescue petting from its tie with intercourse and make it, ideally, a delicate excursion of self-discovery, we must educate young people to recognize other people's phony disguises as well as their own vulnerability.

We must also be realistic about the sexual tensions our culture thrusts on young people by its ideal of long-term educational achievement. We want our children to have high vocational goals, and our technology often demands a college education to reach them. Marriage must thus be postponed to a time long past the peak of their sexual readiness. For this reason, petting is a game they are forced to play, especially if they believe that sexual intercourse is morally wrong. Of course, for college students who have accepted a relaxed moral attitude toward intercourse, petting will not be a big problem; they can use it simply as foreplay to intercourse if the situation progresses toward

133

it. But for young people who are involved in a lengthy education and want to live up to a Christian ideal regarding intercourse, petting in some form will be a likely compromise.

For them, petting can be either a means of creative growth in responsible freedom or a compulsive exercise in frustration. Which one it becomes will depend on both the character of the young people involved and the attitudes they have toward sex. If they have a mature ability to criticize their own motives and recognize their own impulses, they have half the battle won. And if, in addition, they can get beyond the notion that the inevitable goal of sexual exploration is intercourse, they can be in a state of mind to relate to another person sexually without suspecting that every intimacy is only another stage toward liftoff. Lacking character and lacking a realistic view of sexual relationships, they will tend to be compulsive about petting. A girl may feel compelled to repay her date for an expensive evening by "tolerating" his fondling; though many young people have outgrown this kind of bargaining, it is still part of the deal in many places. Young people often feel compelled to pet, as well as to have intercourse, just because "someone expects it of them." And, no matter how they think about intercourse, they are all infected with the virus of a commercial culture that makes sexual attractiveness the motive for almost everything they buy, wear, or do; and they often feel like failures if they do not have a chance to do some petting. So petting easily becomes compulsive. Compulsive petting is a failure of freedom in the Christian person, and it is likely to become an experience of both frustration and guilt. The more a young person assumes that petting is only foreplay to intercourse, the more compulsive he will be when he does it — and the more frustration and guilt he will feel. But petting as a means of exploring personal relationships, done freely and responsibly, can be an experience of growth in understanding and loving.

Is there, then, a simple moral answer to the question of petting? The answer must be no. Is petting a responsible activity within a Christian framework? The answer must be loud and clear: "It all depends." It is morally appropriate within the limits of responsibility toward one's self and respect toward the other. One thing we have to avoid is the morally silly notion that anyone who manages to avoid penetration has kept himself free from fornication. "Technical chastity" is only an escape from responsibility. A person who pets, perhaps to orgasm, but preserves "virginity," is not for that reason upholding the Christian sexual standard. But we must avoid the equally false notion that petting is really on the same level as intercourse, as though the only difference is the technical matter of the location of the genitals.

The morality of petting depends on the degree of personal involvement and commitment between the two persons. "Light petting" could be wrong for some couples; very "heavy petting" could be right for others. Petting has a lot of built-in risks; the risks are both psychological and moral. Living as we do in an atmosphere saturated with propaganda that almost compels young people into sexual permissiveness, we cannot ignore the fact of risk. Nor, however, can we prevent young people from accepting it. If we take biblical sexual morality more seriously than we do our distrust of young persons in this area, we will have to say this about the morality of petting: there are no hard-and-fast rules. Since this is true, the task of moral educators — parents, pastors, leaders — is to work at the development of Christian sensitivity, Christian responsibility, and Christian freedom.

A young person's inclination to be responsible in petting depends on what he brings to it. No one makes love without bringing a self into the encounter; and whether that encounter is creative or destructive depends pretty much on what has gone into the making of that self beforehand. Long before a young man first touches the erotic areas of a young woman's body, he has created a structure of life-experience in which petting is somehow going to fit. What values has he learned to prize? What are the things he most deeply wants for himself? How does he arrange his list of desires? Which takes first place in his life? What goals has he set for himself? Has he learned regard for other persons — his friends, his family, his idols? How does he feel toward himself? What does he expect from himself and for himself in the future? In short, what sort of character is beginning to emerge, and what scenario is he writing with his life? This is really the question that is going to be answered in his petting experience.

A young person takes into his petting a perspective of himself in relationship with other persons who are significant to his life. If he is a Christian, he sees himself somehow related to Jesus Christ. How he fits into his person-filled environment is bound to influence his view of himself. Is he just a person on his own, or does he somehow see an extension of these other significant persons within his own life? If he does, he will carry his sense of identity with others into his sexual relations. Furthermore, he will have developed a view of his own body: either he sees his body as a package that merely wraps a soul inside of it or he sees it as an extension of his very self. If he accepts his body as an extension of his deepest self, he will sense that his whole self ought to be involved in fondling another person's body. And he will also be aware that the body he is fondling is a whole person. Will this adventure in love-making be segregated from what he thinks is his real self, or will it be integrated into the picture that he sees when he thinks about what he is and wants to be? The answer to this question will determine whether petting is likely to be an integrated personal, and thus responsible, experience.

Young persons who come to petting with a solid sense of their own worth are in pretty good shape to be responsible in petting. They will not have to make conquests in order to convince themselves that they are worth something; nor will they have to get self-esteem by the discovery that they are able to excite another person into sexual response. A successful adventure into love-making at this stage is bound to be ego-boosting. This is perfectly good. But persons whose initial anxiety is not balanced by a basic self-esteem are going to be very tempted to turn petting into a compulsive lunge toward the acceptance and self-love they lack. I strongly suspect that most compulsive petting is a search for a self that can be sure of its own lovableness.

A young person's feelings about himself are also likely to have a good deal to do with how he regards the other person. Can he respect the body of the other person as an extension of his/her selfhood? And can he approach petting with a deep regard and concern for him/her as a person? Is there an application of God's regard for personal worth to his regard for the other person? If so, he will ask — even before petting — what do I want for and from him/her? Where am I in relationship to this person with his/her own special and deep ego needs? With questions like these on the edges of their consciousness, young men and women will be less likely to use their partners' bodies as tools for their own ego needs. And both will be much more likely to recognize the exit signs, to sense the right moment for drawing back. As each stage of petting pushes them into the next, the submerged personal question will subtly assert itself: what do we really want with each other?

Another crucial factor of selfhood that one brings to petting is the supply of interests he has cultivated. If one comes to petting with a mind vacuum, with no concerns about the world to share, no hopes to relate, no vital and intense interests to communicate, petting is likely to become a sheer refuge from boredom. For the empty mind and spirit, there is little to give and accept but the sexual arousal of body contact. And when this is the case, petting becomes compulsive. A vacuum in a relationship is going to be filled; and when two vacuous body-persons begin the petting route, the vacuum will be filled by an ever increasing tempo of physical contact. No stage in petting is ever wholly satisfying; each new stage is exciting for the first time, but very soon becomes the launching pad to the next. And where the only thing going into the relationship is physical desire, only a *fear* of going on is likely to abort the process. And, in sex, even a very imperfect love casts out fear.

What I have been leading up to is this: the secret of responsible petting is responsive personhood. There are no exact rules to apply. The real question about petting is the question about the sort of person one is, the sort of person he wants to be, and the sort of person he expects others to want him to be. Within this framework, the maturing person will ask: where does petting, or where does this stage of petting, fit into my personal autobiography?

SELF-PETTING

Stretching a point, we can talk about masturbation as a form of self-petting. Of course, there is a big difference. For one thing, only one person is involved. This makes masturbation less risky than petting, because there is hardly a way it can be used to exploit another person. But it also makes masturbation more suspect, because it is sexual release with no communication of affection to another person. Another difference is that a masturbating youngster almost always intends to reach orgasm — usually as quickly as possible. But it is like petting in this sense: it involves manipulating erogenous areas of the body without having sexual intercourse. People used to invent horrible reasons to make youngsters feel guilty about masturbating. Today the reverse is true. People worry now about how to let them masturbate without having guilt feelings about it. The mood today is that masturbation is all right; only the guilt is bad. I do not want to dispute the modern attitude. But I do think we should examine the reasons why most youngsters in our society *do* feel guilty about masturbating. What is the connection between the guilt and the act itself?

The traditional way to assess masturbation has been to focus on its aloneness. As homosexual acts distort the heterosexual direction of sex, masturbation aborts the interpersonal direction. Masturbation cannot be a venture in communication between two persons because it is a private affair, like talking to oneself sexually. It is solo sex, and solo sex is self-centered, aimed purely at selfish gratification and release. What should we say about this? If masturbation were a permanent sexual life-style, it would be a distortion of what sex is meant to be. It would be a long-term escape from the responsibilities and joys of sexual union. But we must not, it seems to me, come down too hard on masturbation for its self-centeredness. There is nothing wrong with seeking self-satisfaction in sex: every person entering sexual union wants satisfaction for himself as well as for the other. Erotic love is by nature a very self-centered drive; it is always a reaching toward another for self-fulfillment. This is not wrong — unless our own needs compel us to ignore the needs of the other. So the fact that masturbation is a way of satisfying one's own self does not make it wrong. It would be wrong only if it were a lifelong substitute for interpersonal sex.

For most youngsters masturbation is a passing phase of sexual release. They usually move beyond its secret aloneness into a search for intimacy with another person. Masturbation is the adolescent's answer to an obvious problem. As a person he is unripe for serious intimacy with anyone; socially, he is prevented from responsible intimacy by his need for education and financial status. Meanwhile, his sexual needs and abilities are ripening very fast. Masturbation is a ready solution to the unequal tempo of his biological, personal, and social growth. Because nature does not keep things synchronized, youngsters need an easy way to compensate. The fact that biology and personal growth are out of step is complicated by yet another feature of adolescent life. At this time youngsters are absorbed in themselves, struggling desperately to find out who and what they really are. Their preoccupation with themselves coincides with their maturing sex

139

needs. So, once again, we may expect them to turn to their own genitals for sexual self-discovery.

Moral concern about masturbation must focus on its role in the youngster's total development toward a wholesome hetero-sexual life. For parents this is a question of how they can help a youngster see and accept masturbation as part of his growth as a human being. How will masturbation fit into the rest of his normal development? Will he masturbate with a depressing sense of shame, keeping it furtively separate from his acceptable net-work of activities, as a dark and terrible secret? Or will he naturally include it within the normal range of his activities along with baseball, television, and homework? Or are these unrealistic op-tions? Masturbation touches a deep, mysterious, and agitating side of his self that none of the other things he does can match. It is bound to be unsatisfying no matter how nonchalant he is expected to be about it. It always leaves something lacking. A person masturbates with a deep need for another person to fulfill his sexuality. So it is unrealistic to suppose that we can teach youngsters to accept masturbation the same way they accept Little League baseball.

The secret lies, I think, in having living models of healthy, happy, heterosexual relations. If the young person can gradually adopt good heterosexual models as the ideal toward which he is also groping, he may learn to cope with the unsatisfying, unful-filling, even empty experience of masturbation as a phase en route to a better way of sexual fulfillment. He needs to learn that the feeling of emptiness after masturbating is not guilt, but only incompleteness. In this way masturbation can be accepted, along with its frustrations, as a temporary plateau for his sexuality. It is not morally wrong, but neither is it personally sufficient. It is not on the same casual level with other activities, but neither is it a terrible secret sin.

But people who masturbate often do become compulsive about it. This is a deeper problem than the sheer fact of sexual self-manipulation. Why does masturbation become a compulsive habit? Why do youngsters often feel they cannot help themselves, that they are caught in a trap? Why do they swear to themselves again and again that they will not masturbate, but do it again and again anyway? The guilt, the shame, the sense of doing something evil does not keep them from masturbating. Is it possible that the compulsion to masturbate is connected with the very guilt one feels in masturbating?

I am going to suggest that compulsive masturbation is a form of self-punishment. We used to call it self-abuse, but we meant only a physical abuse. Nobody calls it that anymore. But it may just be a form of self-abuse — not of one's body but of the soul. Let me explain what I mean. Many youngsters bear a heavy load of vague, unattached guilt. They cannot locate any concrete horrendous evil in their lives, but they still feel vaguely guilty. They need something specific on which to fasten their feelings, and, since their guilt feelings are already fuzzily related to uneasiness about their sexuality, what better peg is there to hang their guilt feelings on than masturbation? They already feel somewhat empty and unsatisfied about masturbation; and it is very easy to translate this feeling into guilt. So they masturbate and punish themselves afterward with cruel self-accusations. At least here they can connect that inner feeling of reprobation and guilt with something terribly real to them, and then go back to it the next day so that they can keep the guilt-trip going.

This may sound farfetched, but we must remember that there is usually a hidden reason behind compulsive behavior. If masturbation were only a self-centered act of pleasure, it would not become as compulsive as it often is. But as a means of degrading one's self in order to justify one's own feeling of guilt, it can easily become a compulsive self-punishment. The answer to this problem is grace. The answer is not to feed a young person's compulsion by encouraging him in his suspicion that he is guilty for masturbating; this will only lead to more compulsive masturbation. It is, I think, more difficult for adolescents to accept grace than it is for adults. Therefore, it is all the more imperative for Christian parents to mediate God's grace to their children. Children have to taste and feel the grace of God through human grace: the youngster can deeply feel God's acceptance only if he also feels it through his parents. I am personally convinced that the only answer to compulsive masturbation is the discovery that one need not punish himself with it. And that discovery is grace.

In summary, then, most adolescents are likely to masturbate to some extent — given the uneven tempo of their personal development. Christian moral response will not bother too much with the theoretical question of whether masturbation as such is an evil. The moral response to masturbation will be one of asking how we can help youngsters pass through this phase into a responsible heterosexual life. We will want to help them integrate this temporary activity, with all its unsatisfying after-feelings, into their struggles toward mature and whole personhood. I think it naive to suppose that we can rid youngsters of all uneasiness and shame connected with masturbation. But we can help them avoid getting into the compulsive rut of spiritual self-abuse. And the basic means that God has wondrously made available is the assurance of his grace, the confidence of his total and unconditional acceptance.

PART THREE

SEX AND
MARRIED PEOPLE

CHAPTER EIGHT

Creative Fidelity

The sexual life of human beings receives its fulfillment in marriage; this is a nonnegotiable item of biblical sexual morality. A permanent and total partnership gives human sexuality its moral environment as well as its greatest promise for integration with the whole of a rich personal life. We can assume that the true relationship between marriage and sex is not like the relationship between a corral and a lusty bull: marriage is not just an enclave to keep our sexual impulses from becoming roaming lusts. Marriage is not just a God-given lid to clamp down on an impulse that, left free to roam, could reduce life to chaos, or, suppressed, could leave a person "aflame with passion" (I Cor. 7:9). In marriage, the radical self-giving, the unique self-exposure, and the unreserved sharing of selves that sex really aims at is given its best chance for success. Marriage is not just for the control of sex; it is for the liberation and fulfillment of sex.

If we think positively about marriage, we need to think positively about fidelity. The Christian morality of sex is often boiled down to continence outside of marriage and fidelity within marriage. But in that view fidelity too often amounts to putting a leash on lust; fidelity then is only a successful negation. But

145

fidelity is first of all an affirmation. Keeping faith obligates us to act out a positive commitment. The prohibition of adultery in the Seventh Commandment has a positive base: its negative phrasing really says, "Thou shalt be faithful." And faithfulness is affirmative action. Fidelity certainly involves the location of one's genitals, but it also stretches far beyond: it extends into the whole marital relationship.

Married people are obligated to be faithful; this is the given. But what are they called to be faithful *to?* Marriage has many dimensions, and a partner's fidelity involves all of them. One might say that the obligation of fidelity means faithfulness to the marriage vow. There is truth to this. The Seventh Commandment could perhaps be translated: "You shall not violate your vow." But we will need to ask what sort of thing a marriage vow is, and whether one is really faithful to it if all he manages to do is "forsake all others" and "cleave only to" his spouse.

Fidelity could also mean faithfulness to a vocation. Marriage is a calling in life, a station one accepts. To be married means that a partnership has been formed to serve others — friends, neighbors, and community. But we will have to ask what sort of service is involved. Fidelity could also mean faithfulness to a person, to one's partner as a human being. To fulfill the duty of fidelity would then mean to dedicate oneself to a life of creative ministry for the well-being of a partner. We will have to ask about the meaning of this. Fidelity also could obligate us to the development of a personal relationship, to the growth, not just of two individuals, but of the relationship between them. This would bring fidelity out of sterile confinement to sexual monogamy into a dynamic commitment to a growing personal relationship. It may also be that fidelity is an obligation to all of these, none in isolation from the others.

A man or woman can be just too busy, too tired, too timid, too prudent, or too hemmed in with fear to be seriously tempted by an adulterous affair. But this same person can be a bore at home, callous to the delicate needs of his partner. He or she may be too prudish to be an adventuresome lover, but too cowardly to be in honest communication and too busy to put himself out for anything more than a routine ritual of personal commitment. He/she may be able to claim that he/she never cheated; but he/she may not be able to claim that he/she was ever really honest. He/she may never have slipped outside the marriage; but he/she may never have tried to grow along with his/her partner into a deep, personal relationship of respect and regard within marriage. His/her brand of negative fidelity may be an excuse for letting the marriage fall by neglect into dreary conformity to habit and, with that, into a dull routine of depersonalized sex. I am not minimizing the importance of negative fidelity; but anyone who thinks that morality in marriage is fulfilled by avoiding an affair with a third party has short-circuited the personal dynamics of fidelity.

1. A MODEL OF FIDELITY

The Christian concept of fidelity is based on the model offered to us by the marriage between God and his people. The fidelity of God is the example that gives positive thrust to the fidelity demanded of husbands and wives. If we use this model, we will avoid the sterile, passive caricature of fidelity that is mere absence of adultery. We will have a picture of someone who makes a solemn vow to enduring partnership and whose fidelity is measured in terms of creative love for his partner.

God did make a commitment, a vow to be a God to his people and to accept them through thick and thin as his own. He came one day as a virtual stranger to vow to a common Chaldean, a wholly unlikely partner, that he would commit his whole self to him and his community forever. The long story of God's marriage to Israel is the story of God's fidelity to that vow. He allowed neither his partner's infidelity nor the attractiveness

147

of other candidates for his love to be an excuse for reneging on his commitment. All that we read of his justice and faithfulness in the Old Testament is focused on his fidelity to the vow once made. His fidelity was often abused by his partner; it even became a pretext for taking his favor for granted. But he overlooked even this gross presumption on his fidelity to the marriage vow: "And I will betroth you to me for ever; I will betroth you to me in righteousness and in justice, in steadfast love, and in mercy. I will betroth you to me in faithfulness; and you shall know the Lord" (Hos. 2:21-22).

God's fidelity is much more, however, than loyalty to a bargain he could not break. His constancy to Israel had a broader base than commitment to a contract between himself and a select group of people. God's fidelity was focused on his human partner: what he sought was Israel's good. What he seeks now is the church's good. His vow is not simply a legalistic loyalty to a bargain, but it is a commitment to the health and welfare, in all dimensions, of his partner. Fidelity, as modeled by God, concentrates on the total well-being of the other member of the partnership. Throughout the relationship God is bent on the freedom of his partner, and bent on the partner's growth into genuine maturity in Christ. Thus, as it is mirrored in God, fidelity means something positive, dynamic, and person-directed.

Finally, God's fidelity is to a relationship. He wants the welfare and growth of his human partner, but always for the other in relationship to himself. Once committed, he no longer lived as a God unto himself; and once committed, Israel and the church were no longer to live as people unto themselves. They were to find their identity — as God and as human community — in terms of their relationship. God's faithfulness from the beginning has been a loyalty to the relationship that he created, to nurture it, to make it grow and flourish as both partners entered more deeply into it. In all the ebb and flow of changing times and circumstances, the Lord of history is faithful to his commitment

148

to make that relationship an effective one — through prayer, worship, and all the surprising encounters that God and his people have in history together.

Moreover, once begun, God's partnership with Israel was to be a means of blessing "to all the families of the earth." He "got married" to one nation in order to take up a vocation of service and worldly concern for the salvation of all nations. And fidelity *within* the partnership included the vocation of redemptive ministry to those *outside* the partnership. His marriage partner, as the Old Testament relates it, constantly shortchanged this extramarital vocation; Israel wanted to reduce God to a partner whose fidelity was directed exclusively to the marriage, and to reduce the partnership to a nuclear twosome with no open doors to the world outside. But God's vocation was to the world — through the special partnership.

So, in summary, we can say that God's faithfulness is dynamic and positive, always geared to the future, never a matter of being stuck with a past vow, and focused on much more than mere absence of spiritual adultery. It is fidelity to the vow; but the vow's whole point was commitment to the welfare of the partner, commitment to the relationship between himself and his partner, and commitment of the partnership to the world outside it.

2. FIDELITY TO A VOW

In Christian cultures people traditionally begin their partnership with a vow, made to each other, while calling on God and the community as witnesses. The vow includes a commitment to stay together in exclusive sexual partnership. The moral obligation of fidelity, then, entails loyalty to one's vow, which fixes the partnership in solemn personal commitment. A vow is an act of trust in the face of an uncertain future. It is a wager on the unseen tomorrow. People's feelings toward one another flutter like flags in a variable wind, and the personal bond at the center of marriage is fragile and fluid. Communion between a man and a woman is always lived out somewhere outside of Eden. Each goes into marriage with expectations that never perfectly match the expectations the other person has; neither partner lives up to virginal dreams. Most often neither is fully aware of what the other partner expects from the marriage, and therefore both can be disappointed. Besides, what we want from marriage changes as we change. And no two partners change on exactly the same schedule. So they grow apart. But looming in from the past is a vow once made: in the teeth of future contingencies a vow was made freely and solemnly before God. And fidelity is a moral demand put on marriage partners to keep faith with the vow once made.

Literal seriousness about vows is not in tune with the temper of our time. For one thing, a serious vow of permanence in the face of all the unforeseeable problems is extremely difficult to make. Many people are psychically incapable of making a sincere vow to exclusiveness and permanence. They may want a lasting marriage; they may hope for a happy marriage; but to commit themselves to a situation that will last "until death do us part" is simply asking more than they can give. Vow-making has become a victim of "future shock"; rapid change has sapped us of the psychic vitality to think in terms of permanence.

Moreover, marriage vows are no longer taken literally as vows. They have really come to mean: "for as long as the marriage seems to be working out well," or "as long as love shall last." This does not mean that people are sheer hypocrites when they recite the vows. We must face up to the realities of the culture in which people get married. Most of the cultural support structures that once made vow-keeping fairly easy have been undermined or destroyed. And, besides being characterized by the loss of community support and psychic power, ours is a time when the "good" marriage has become the criterion of whether a marriage should continue at all. What a "good" marriage is depends on everyone's own dreams, but it centers on the personal satisfaction of those involved. In any case, people's moral power to make meaningful vows in our time is limited. We must be realistic about this fact when we ask everyone getting married to speak them.

Apart from the problem of *making* vows, the mere *keeping* of vows has its own limits. If fidelity were merely stubborn loyalty to a vow once made, it would miss the authentic meaning of fidelity. A disillusioned husband might grit his teeth in moral heroics, plow along in a marriage that is filled with conflict and hate, and out of sheer loyalty to a vow manage to avoid sexual contact outside of marriage. Thus fidelity to a vow would be a cold moral stubbornness. And it could mean no more than that two people stick it out together in an empty shell called a marriage. Two people can be faithful to their vow without ever making of marriage the kind of personal union that God had in mind when he talked of two people becoming "one flesh."

But we want nonetheless to affirm the importance of fidelity to the vow. A vow is a commitment, made freely, which does bind a person to another. Vows tell us that life has an intentional side to it — as do love and marriage. Contrary to a good deal of Freudian and behavioristic depreciation of human intention, we must affirm that life is sustained by the wills of persons. The question is whether we are passive bondslaves to forces beyond our control — either forces coming from outside us or those coming from somewhere in our subconscious. Or are we, at some deep point in our consciousness, also masters of our futures. To make a vow is to say that "for better or for worse" we will not let circumstances or fate determine the future of our marriage. To make a vow for the future is to affirm that we can will to make our marriages better than they are, good enough at least to keep alive the promise that they can be very good. Fidelity to a vow can be willed, and as an act of intention, can carry two people through lean and troubled times in their personal relationship.

151

Couples are sometimes tempted to see themselves as children of fate, and their marriage *fated* to shipwreck. I am not saying that every marriage situation contains fertile seeds of hope; no doubt some are beyond salvage. But in our current frame of mind it is too easy to give oneself up to the fates and call it quits too soon. It is to people of such frail resolve that we ought to talk about vows in a positive sense as a moral obligation. They made a vow freely. Their vow brought them into a status for which they are responsible. The marriage is a fact they created by their will, and their will is still a lively component of their situation. If the Christian gospel, and not determinism, is true, then married partners can will and act to make a better marriage out of a bad one just as they willed to create the marriage in the first place. Loyalty to a vow cannot turn a commitment to endurance into a happy marriage; but intentional faithfulness to a promise once made can sustain the possibility for a re-creation of the marriage. This is a time not to minimize but to affirm the deep meaning of vow-making.

The vow stands as a reminder that marriage is based on more than eros. Eros is the pull of desire, the promise of satisfaction; it is the lure of fulfillment and the beckoning light of joy. But eros waxes and wanes, and its power is very fragile. However, a marriage in which the flame of eros has dwindled to ashes is still possibly a marriage with a future. For eros can be, with the right will, revived. In the meantime, the memory of a solemn vow to see the partnership through "worse as well as better" can be an invisible buttress until eros lives again.

3. FIDELITY TO A CALLING

Marriage as a vocation may sound like a sexual version of the Protestant work ethic. Yet it is an authentic dimension of marriage. A revival of the concept of marriage as a vocation is needed on two fronts: people who think of marriage as only an intimate relationship which they chose for their own fulfillment need to know that marriage is a calling; and people who think of marriage as an institution, a status that merely binds two people legally, also need to know that marriage is a calling. To think and feel that marriage is a vocation strikes at two unrealistic notions about marriage: (1) the notion that marriage is an *ad hoc* private arrangement depending wholly on the affection of the people involved, and (2) the notion that marriage is an objective "estate" in which two people are confined. Marriage as a calling is better than both concepts, because a calling summons the partnership to a future that is better than the present.

Marital fidelity is a commitment to the possibilities of the future. God always intends a marriage to be better than it is. No marriage can perfectly match the honest intimacy and shared responsibility that God intends; no marriage is the creatively helpful relationship that God wants. What God had in mind for marriage is, on this earth, always a promise of what can be and therefore a calling to work toward the promise. There is such a thing as marital *status*. Every person who gets married is initiated into a new status in his life. A husband is no longer just an individual: he is a partner in a sexually rooted union. Each woman is no longer just an individual woman, but the partner of a man. To say that marriage is a status into which we enter is to say that God himself has created a partnership, so that the continuation of the marriage is not up to human choice and desire alone. Two people chose each other as partners; but God willed the partnership they enter.

We also know that the sacred status can be in reality a secular shell that houses a callous and hostile relationship. To breathe life into the notion of status, we have to think of it as a *station*, a calling that ties us to the responsibility of making the marriage serve its purpose. Bonhoeffer spoke of this in a wedding sermon that he wrote in prison and never had a chance to deliver in person. Notice how he accepts the notion of status and yet turns it in the direction of vocation:

> Marriage is more than your love for each other. It has a higher dignity and power, for it is God's holy ordinance. . . . In your love you see only the heaven of your happiness, but in marriage you are placed at a post of responsibility towards the world and mankind. Your love is your own private possession, but marriage is something more than personal — it is a status, an office . . . that joins you together in the sight of God and man.

Two people also become partners in service for others. The marriage status is really a vocation that is directed toward the world. As a partnership, two people can serve other people better than they could as separate individuals. An open marriage can mean that the marriage has doors open to the world. Marriage is a vocation in this way: it is not a calling for everyone to get married, but a calling for those who do to make a marriage an active partnership of service to others. For some, the others will be found in the neighborhood; for others, it may be a larger community; for still others, it may be the church. How a marriage serves the world beyond the nuclear partnership must be decided according to each situation and in keeping with the abilities of each couple. But fidelity means that partners ask themselves what good their partnership is to others.

Marriage is also a calling in a more inner-directed sense; it has a reference to the future possibilities of marriage itself. Entering marriage is actually moving toward marriage. We are married in a technical sense the moment the preacher says we are "man and wife." But we are actually just accepting the calling to work *toward* the reality the Bible teasingly calls "one flesh." In this sense, we are forever *becoming* married, always on the way toward a real marriage, always moving toward the personal unity that the institutional unity is meant to sustain. What we are saying is that the calling of marriage is a calling to keep working and striving toward the creative partnership that marriage can be.

Fidelity — far more than staying clear of extramarital affairs — is a response to the vocation to make the legal marriage a real marriage. The call does not come as a voice in the night; the call comes out of the matrix of every day's common demands and every day's potential for creating a better relationship out of an injured and gasping one. Where we hear the calling is in the breakdowns every marriage suffers. The call does not come merely as a law laid down in the Bible, but as a challenge hidden in the ingredients of marriage itself; it comes whenever failures of communication occur, whenever one partner is left weeping for understanding, or whenever the partnership groans under a load of guilt. Then it comes with a summons: heal the wounds and make the marriage real again.

Not everyone has the calling for marriage. But once married, we receive that calling inevitably. And it is a calling that we are not free to ignore. We are free to respond to it in our way, which may be different from anyone else's way; but we are not free to close our ears to it. This is why we are not free to get a divorce whenever we think our marriage is not working to our satisfaction. Whether we like to think of it in these terms or not, we are in fact set at a station where God calls us into the future of the partnership we are in. And we are not at liberty to leave that station whenever we wish.

4. FIDELITY TO PERSONS

We must now get closer to the center of marriage. A marriage is a partnership rooted in sexual desire, an arrangement for the good of the persons involved. At the core, fidelity in partnership is commitment to an ongoing, dynamic, changing, sensitive facing off of two people bent on the total well-being of each other. And each is faithful to the extent that he is dedicated to the constant growth, healing, and regrowth of the other person. Fidelity, in short, is person-centered.

I cannot claim to meet the demands of fidelity if I am less than faithful to my wife's total welfare. This must mean at the outset that I am dedicated to my wife's freedom from me so that she can become a full person in her own right. Nor can I be faithful to her unless I am free to be a real, independent person myself. There is indeed a risk here: independence can slide into indifference or competition. But there is less risk here than there is when one partner is only a shadow of the other. A man and his shadow are not partners any more than are a man and the image he sees in the mirror. Partnerships require independence within unity. So I cannot be faithful to my wife unless I encourage her to be free *from* me so that she can be free *for* me.

Fidelity calls for a partner to work for the other's freedom so that she/he can be "free in Christ" for partnership. This means that no one has a right to give himself unreservedly; he has an obligation to give himself to the other person's total well-being, but not to give himself totally. Total self-giving, generous as it may seem, is destructive of marriage because it saps a partner of the creative independence he/she needs in order to contribute himself/herself to the other person. In order to give one's self, there must be a genuine self to give. Thus the condition for self-giving is self-assertion; every partner has a duty of fidelity to himself/herself and, equally, a duty of fidelity to let the other be a real self.

I should say something here to qualify what I said above concerning fidelity to a calling. The irony of fidelity to one aspect of marriage is that it can be an excuse for infidelity to another aspect. For example, two persons can turn their marriage into a service agency for others while neglecting fidelity to each other's individuality. Nowhere is this more likely than in the marriage of

a clergyman, though it is also true of all marriages that are partnerships in service. Here a man's fidelity to a calling combines
with his wife's total self-giving to produce infidelity to the woman
as a person. A minister is tempted to think of his marriage in
terms of the service both partners can give to the church; the
minister's wife is tempted to think of her role as self-giving to the
minister in his ministry to the church. So she is cheated at several
ends: she is cheated out of the fidelity that her husband owes her
as a person, and she is cheated out of her own selfhood, which
she gives away so that she can be a shadow of her husband.
Ministers' wives are frequently abused as persons while they share
the "joys of ministry" to others.

Fidelity becomes a moral achievement when it is person-
directed; it is less moral when it is function-based. A woman may
avoid adultery because marriage functions as a secure nest for
her. A man may avoid adultery because marriage is a useful
function in his business. Or both may be faithful only because
their marriage provides adequate sexual release. Or they may be
faithful for the sake of the children. These are all functional
reasons for negative fidelity. But positive fidelity is first of all a
dedication to the freedom, the maturity, and the growth of the
other person. Being faithful to one's spouse is not persistent
resistance to the seductions of third persons; it is a positive and
sometimes painful promotion of one's spouse as a free person.
This, I think, was Paul's intent when he said that husbands and
wives should be "subject to one another" (Eph. 5:21). Whatever
Paul's convictions about inequality were, he had a christological
view of person-centered fidelity. The avoidance of adultery could
never satisfy the demands of this fidelity: "Husbands, love your
wives, as Christ loved the church. . . ." (Eph. 5:25). Christ "nour-
ishes and cherishes the church" as if it were himself, and it is "for
this reason" that a man and woman become "one flesh" (Eph.
5:31): in marriage, they are to serve one another as they serve
themselves.

5. FIDELITY TO A RELATIONSHIP

Finally, fidelity means a stubborn dedication to growth in personal relationship. A marriage partnership must have room for individual growth; but at the beating heart of any marriage is the delicate, fragile — often painful — but potentially joyful relationship of two persons face-to-face in personal encounter. The vital core of marriage is the special kind of sexual communion that vibrates on every level — physical, emotional, intellectual, and spiritual. All the institutional dimensions are only the framework for the dynamic center. And if partners are faithful in the complex ways mentioned above, their fidelity will mean a steady dedication to the growth of an honest and open relationship in every dimension.

Fidelity is practiced best with an implicit understanding that the relationship happens *within* a permanent, lifelong structure. But within the structure of permanence, relationships are constantly shifting: they are never stagnant, but grow deeper or become shallower. To be faithful means that we can never lazily accept the present as our fated destiny. For relationships never have to be what they are; they can change. The future has possibilities wherever two willing human beings affirm its possibilities for them. No one can make a claim to faithfulness in marriage if he does not keep the door open to the possibilities that his relationship can be better tomorrow than it is today.

Personal relationships are nourished only through communication, and communication between two people enmeshed in daily preoccupations with jobs, budgets, diapers, and new math can be very difficult to maintain. For one thing, it takes time. It also takes psychic vitality. And, above all, it takes desire. Personal communication is difficult because it is painful for us to talk about what we are feeling; it is much easier to discuss the unbalanced checking account than to discuss how we feel toward each other. But more, it is difficult because when we talk we are not sure what becomes of our message after it is filtered through the receptive apparatus of the person who receives it. That filter is built out of the wishes, fears, and needs — to say nothing of hostilities — of the other person. We seldom hear exactly what the other person says. By the time we have filtered his message through our own system, we have translated it in terms of our own feelings. This has implications for the morality of fidelity. Fidelity will give us the job of finding out what the other person is actually hearing from us and of patiently probing what the other person is actually trying to say.

Couples often give up on communication too early. They decide too soon that their partners cannot understand their needs, their wishes, and their fears. Or they conclude too easily that their partners cannot *bear* to hear their disappointments, their anger, or their frustrations. Or they enjoy the bitter luxury of smoldering anger so much that they do not want to expose it, for fear they may lose their advantage. There are a thousand reasons why partners find it easier to block communication than to restore it. But meanwhile, they are failing to be faithful at a point where marital faithfulness is most vital. People who preach the morality of fidelity in our time will have to worry less about adultery and more about communication. There are moral husbands who can stiffly claim, "I have never been unfaithful," but who are unfaithful to the most obvious marital task they have: the growth of a human relationship in open and respectful communication with their wives. What fidelity calls for is not merely a grim nay-saying to extramarital affairs but a yea-saying to the humble, sensitive, and painful job of keeping the lines of communication open.

This touches most sensitively on what happens in the bedroom. Today partners are properly encouraged to take stock of their sexual relationships. A wife may discover that she is being left out in the cold sexually; a husband may discover that his performance is shabby. Both may secretly consider their life in

159

bed a bore or a chore. But thousands of partners suffer in silence, either because of the inadequacy of their partners or their suspicion of their own abilities. Human beings are the only creatures who can talk while making love; and they are the only ones who can talk *about* it afterward. So fidelity in marriage means that couples ought to ask each other frankly: "How are we doing sexually?" Open communication about sexual performance could lead either or both partners to seek sexual therapy. While it is true that sexual technique cannot create good sexual relationships, bad technique can make them very miserable. But what communication can do best is open one another in sympathy and understanding to each other's needs and fears. And this in turn could do more for good sexual relationships than daily visits to a sex clinic. Or it could be the beginning of a decision to seek out a clinic. Let it be said again: fidelity in marriage is an obligation to keep the door open to future possibilities of better personal relationships.

Stressing the moral obligation of fidelity in this positive sense is a realistic response to a profound change in how people feel about marriage and what they expect from it. Marriage relationships have turned inward on themselves: the quality of personal relationships in marriage has become the crucial question of whether the marriage will survive. In other days, couples had to face outward against threats to physical survival; they had to fight together against nature and competition to keep food on the table. But where hunger or other threats no longer lurk at the threshold of tomorrow, partners have the leisure to demand the luxury of a happy personal relationship together.

The isolation of the nuclear family makes relationship even more crucial: with only husband and wife and a couple of children under the roof, the relationship between partners is the only one there is to worry about. At one time, husband and wife worried about their relationship to parents and other relatives; now they only have themselves. Besides, the nuclear family often exists as an island in a neighborhood of strangers. Few families live within a supporting community of people who care, a community of shared values, morals, and faith that supports the marriage even when the relationship within it has become cold. And fewer marriages exist in a community that has the moral authority to persuade partners to keep trying even when the relationship is personally stifling. The upshot is that marriages stand or fall on the basis of what happens between the two partners in the words, gestures, looks, and silences that communicate love, anger, or indifference to each other. The point of all this is: marriage has become a fragile relationship at the center. So moral obligation must bear on this fragile center.

However, we must think of moral obligation with compassion. Today's married people do not choose the culture they live in; they inherit it. If the community does not support them, this is not the doing of people getting married today. Therefore, to preach obligation these days is to accept the burden of helping people meet their obligations in a creative way. The church, for instance, will have to re-examine its own resources: what can it do to educate married people in communication with each other? For one thing, it can give them occasions to practice it in the company of others. Most people need help in learning how to listen and how to discover what the other person is hearing. And the church community, with its commitment to unconditional grace, ought to be an ideal environment for them to learn these lessons of practical grace.

Our modern emphasis of focusing on personal relationships puts a heavy strain on marriage. For one thing, marriage is almost the only place in our lives where lasting and deep personal relations are possible. In a mobile society, our relationships outside marriages tend to be very fragmentary, short-lived, and shallow; they involve business or sports or some other partial aspect of our lives, without touching on our deepest hurts and hopes. So marriage partners are led to expect and need an enormous personal benefit from their relationships with each other. This is why they become so deeply angry and frustrated when the marriage does not provide that rich personal fulfillment. The problem with marriage today is not that we expect too little from it; the problem is that we have to demand too much from it.

Putting personal relationships at the center of marriage poses one more moral problem in our age; it is the question of "open marriage." Openness of partners to each other is the goal of positive fidelity. The question will arise whether openness can be a door leading to affairs outside the marriage. At this point we must make a critical decision as to whether personal relationships, at the center, are also the essence and ultimate goal of marriage. The quality of personal relationships is measured by very private standards. Each of the partners has his own standards; and his standards are created by his own expectations. This means that the quality of communication and fulfillment is judged from two different perspectives, which are based on two different expectations. Some people need and demand much more than others do; some are utopian while others are realistic; some demand too much while others expect only the possible.

Now let us imagine that, in a given marriage, there is open communication, in which the partners become aware of the fact that one of them is satisfied while the other is unsatisfied. And both are determined to be faithful to the job of creating a better relationship in which both are satisfied more fully. What, then, if they should decide that a sexual affair outside of marriage would contribute to their relationship within their open marriage? If personal relationships are the sole standard, only the practical question of whether an outside "sexual friendship" might help or hurt a relationship would be relevant. It is in this setting that fidelity in the old-fashioned sense is said to be the "false god of a closed marriage." If marriage is defined wholly as personal relationship, then anything that helps the relationship is fair play. The biblical view is that the physical union of sexual relationships is interwoven into the total life-union. This is a nonnegotiable basis for the morality of personal relationships in marriage. The biblical veto of "sexual friendships" outside of marriage, then, is rooted in the unity of sexual and personal relationships within marriage. It is highly doubtful, therefore, that extramarital sexual affairs will ever enrich a personal relationship within marriage.

What we are saying in this section is that personal relationships are at the center but are not the whole of marriage. But there at the center, they are the focus of marital fidelity. Fidelity is a moral summons to make of the living center an ongoing, growing, continuously re-created personal relationship of honest and open communication.

6. FREEDOM THROUGH FIDELITY

Sexual freedom comes into its own in a life of fidelity. A personal partnership, sustained in commitment and supported by a faith that God intends permanence for marriage, is the best environment for sexual freedom. For here alone sexual experience can find the uncluttered trust and personal security to grow into the adventure of sexual discovery. Here, in the atmosphere of total acceptance, sex can be human and thus truly free. The adventures and joys of sexual intercourse can be accepted with wild abandon for all that they promise; some of its disappointments can also be accepted with mild humor. It can be gratefully grasped without expecting paradise, and it can be accepted with patience when it brings us less than was hoped. It can be great without bringing heaven on earth, and it can be less than great without creating a feeling of being cheated. But most of all, within a partnership of mutual fidelity, sexual relationships can be adventures into ever freer, more liberated expressions of love. Sex can be free only within a relationship rooted in something beyond sex; it is most liberated within personal fidelity.

Sexual freedom means *personal* liberation in sexual relationships. It does not mean a license to experience sex with whomever one wants. Sexual freedom in the sense of unlimited opportunity for coitus is a ridiculous self-contradiction. In the most obvious ways, license to have sexual relationships outside of marriage brings with it the loss of freedom: it almost always entails sexual intercourse in furtive, anxious snippets; it always means that sex is experienced with a reservation of large segments of one's life, whereas sexual freedom demands abandon. License for adultery is a license for harassment by the fear of discovery, the plague of living in duplicity, the stifling feeling of being trapped in a risky situation full of threats to one's security. And even in those rare cases in which spouses consent to one another's extramarital affairs, the two partners lose their freedom toward each other: in spite of the bravado of "swingers," they usually are an anxious and self-tortured group. Sexual freedom is the liberty to explore the possibilities of sexual intimacy in the openness of trust, the security of unreserved acceptance, and the assurance of fidelity. Once again, then, fidelity is the key to sexual freedom. The moral obligation to be faithful is really a calling to create the atmosphere for sexual freedom.

However, it must be said at this point that sexual freedom, like every other aspect of Christian freedom, is a vocation as well as a gift. Christ has set us free from the bondage of fear, including the fear of physical intimacy. By his Spirit he gives us the power to enter boldly into the gift of freedom. But freedom in this life is never to be taken for granted; we are moving toward an ever larger expanse of freedom as we move forward into full maturity in Christ. And the life of working and growing fidelity is the best condition for growth into sexual freedom.

Where marriage is seen as a permanent partnership — not an insecure relationship that can be broken at either partner's will — the partners can be freed from dull moralizing and prudish fears of everything they do. "If I love my wife, if I accept marriage as an institution of God, then there comes an inner freedom and certainty of life and action in marriage; I no longer watch with suspicion every step that I take; I no longer call into question every deed that I perform" (Bonhoeffer). Fidelity in this positive sense is the precondition of sexual freedom because it is the liberating setting for sexual adventure. Adventure, surprise, willingness to risk and experiment — these are possible within the basic security of knowing that when two people are married they really are "one flesh."

CHAPTER NINE

Adultery

The total demands of creative fidelity are enough to unsettle any spouse. Has any married person this side of Eden ever been truly faithful? Once we admit that fidelity asks far more than avoiding sexual contact with a third person, we have a whole new set of marriage responsibilities. What makes fidelity such a fluid challenge is that every partner has to work it out on his own — within the broadest guidelines of personal love and concern. There are no stereotypes, simply because the needs of every person are unique. The Bible gives only basic principles for creative fidelity; it does not provide precise models. A faithful husband in Old Testament times might be insensitive or exploitative today; and a faithful wife in Old Testament times might be a bore — or a scandal — today. Every married person must give shape to his fidelity within his own marriage in terms of his own partner.

But adultery seems to be another matter. Adultery is straightforward; it comes to the same thing in any culture. Sexual intercourse with a person who is not one's spouse: this is adultery, plain and simple. At least, until recently we have always thought so. Now many people are not sure. Or, to put it another way, if they are prepared to label extramarital sex as adultery, they are not ready to brand all adultery as morally wrong.

In this chapter, we are going to zero in on the one adulterous act: sexual intercourse outside the fences of marriage. We do not mean that everyone who avoids extramarital sex is faithful. It must be clear by now that we are not victims of genital obsession; that is, we are not making genital insertion a magic moment that separates fidelity from infidelity. But it is one thing to say that one is *not* morally safe if he merely avoids penetration; it is another to say that he might be morally safe, under some circumstances, if he commits adultery. We are taking up where mainline Christian morality brings us: there is something morally special about sexual intercourse. Of course, there is something psychologically special about it too. For that matter, it is special in many ways. But our interest is in morals.

1. WHY PEOPLE COMMIT ADULTERY

Whatever their reasons may be, many married people do move outside of their marriage for sexual experiences. Back in the fifties, Kinsey discovered — to the surprise of many — that fifty percent of the married men interviewed admitted to having had extra-marital sex. Today most experts in the field tell us that the percentage is more like sixty. Kinsey's team reported that twenty-six percent of forty-year-old women had had at least one adventure in adultery. Today social observers tell us that thirty-five percent is a reasonable figure. Some students of marriage (such as Morton Hunt) predict that before long four out of every five husbands will have had sex outside of marriage, if their marriages last more than a few years. And they add that perhaps two out of three wives will. The fascinating question is — why?

We could, of course, dismiss it as lust and degeneration. It could be that more and more people are simply throwing off restraint and following their fleshly desires. There is some truth to this. But it will not explain why so *many* American spouses are looking for sexual experience outside their marriages. People have always had sexual drives, and none of us is a stranger to lust. But why are so many breaking out of their marriages into adulterous affairs in our time? Our chief interest is in the right and wrong of sexual behavior; but we cannot issue judgments without also trying to understand the reasons. So we will spend a little time trying to capture some of the complicated reasons why people actually do seek out or drift into sexual experience with people other than their spouses. The reasons for adultery are as many as there are adulterers. We cannot put every adulterer in the same moral or psychological category, but we can point to some factors that contribute to adultery. Some of them are external and some internal: some come from our environment; some come from inside of us. And they are interconnected. Our environment contributes to what we feel, and what we feel helps create our environment. But we can roughly separate them.

A. External Encouragement

Our environment, the atmosphere we breathe emotionally, no longer supports sexual monogamy. On the contrary, it pushes people away from it. It is true that there are still many people who resist environmental pressures. Christian life still calls people to turn away from the blandishments of an apostate culture. And many — maybe most — do. But it is still a fact that our environment has encouraged people to take the lid off their sexual needs and urges. At one time, the American scene provided all sorts of props for fidelity and erected fences for lust and sexual need. Neighbors cared and watched; the church admonished and threatened; friends frowned; pregnancy was a real threat. And there was not the media exposure urging us to consider our sexual desires sexual rights. But much of that has changed. I will sketch a few of the currents in our social situation that make adultery attractive and inviting.

1) *The Sexualized Atmosphere*

Everyone is aware that our society puts a premium on sexual fulfillment, not on stable institutions. We are nagged into believing that there is no personal fulfillment without sexual satisfaction. Every popular magazine, most films, and many commercial advertisements make us acutely conscious of our sexuality and our sexual potential and desires. Our ethos is sexually supercharged. This means that married people, once content with stability and security, are now pressured into asking disturbing questions about their own sexual needs and wants.

2) *Sexual Convenience*

We are mobile: we can get away easily to places where we will not be seen. We are affluent: we can pay for the secret lunches and motel rooms. We are free from worry about pregnancy: we have the pill. Convenient adultery is simply within more people's reach than ever before.

3) *Sexual Contact*

Men and women who are married are meeting many more sexually interesting people. Women have become successful in jobs that once were occupied only by males. Men and women meet each other on a free and equal basis. And not all of them are prepared to handle new contacts with sexually available people.

4) *Community Erosion*

We no longer live in neighborhoods where people know us. Our acquaintances and friends no longer care that much about our moral behavior; we have learned not to be our brothers' or sisters' keepers. Our churches have lost their moral clout; furthermore, community pressure and community support have been whittled away. The loss of community life means that the burden has fallen on the partners themselves. And many are not able to cope with the freedom and alienation that the loss of community inflicts on them.

5) *The Romantic Marriage*

Once it was all right to marry for security, comfort, and responsible parenthood. Now we are considered unromantic and calculating if we marry for anything less than erotic desire. This means that we expect personal fulfillment through marriage; and sexual fulfillment is a large part of the package. We are expected to cultivate, celebrate, and voluptuously enjoy sexual life together for our own sakes. But once the experience gets dull or frustrating, some people find that marriage is not, after all, romantic enough. Marriages rooted in erotic desire tend to drive people outside marriage for love when the flames of passion have turned to the ashes of resentment.

These are a few of the externals in our environment that encourage adultery. They wind up the inner springs of sexual need on the one hand; and they break down the fences that used to confine sexual needs on the other. They make adultery easier, and they encourage it besides. We will now take a quick look at some of the inner pressures.

B. Inner Pressures

People are vulnerable for many reasons; no one gets involved in adultery for any single reason. Life is too complicated for that. Every married person who has had an affair is driven and pulled by a legion of conflicting needs and drives. Yet there are some things that many people have in common. I am going to mention a few of them. Taking a cue from psychology, I will take the risk of distinguishing between two categories of inner pressures: sick and healthy. This is a risk because some readers will interpret healthy to mean good and sick to mean bad. All I mean by a healthy pressure is that the people who feel it are not necessarily neurotic. I am also going to list separate inner pressures felt by men and by women. This is also a risk — the risk of male arrogance or ignorance. Women readers will have to judge for themselves whether I am making sense.

1) Sick Pressures

a) Anger

Anger is a hard driver. It pushes people toward any act that can punish the person toward whom their anger is directed. Unresolved anger can pressure a husband or wife into an affair with another person in order to punish a spouse for all his/her failures. The angry person is not falling in love with a third person; he is falling in anger against his spouse. A wife may feel that she is always giving, never getting. Perhaps her husband has been unfaithful, insensitive, or brutal. What better way to punish him than by getting involved with another man? A husband may feel that he is put upon — always providing, always faithful, always extending himself to take care of his wife's needs while he gets little in either emotional or sexual satisfaction. What more effec-

172

tive way does he have to get even than to have an affair with an attractive woman? This is a sick pressure because anger can be dealt with in a constructive way. And it is sick because it uses one person sexually in order to punish another.

b) Self-Hatred

Self-deprecation is a cruel pressure toward adultery. It pushes a person to get involved with someone who will not judge him for his failures. Some people have a very low opinion of themselves: they demand too much and condemn themselves for not meeting their own impossible demands. They walk under an umbrella of shame and guilt. Moreover, they project their own self-hatred into the minds of their spouses: they believe that their spouses must be as intolerant and unforgiving of them as they are of themselves. Since they dare not reveal their blemishes within the marriage, they are pressured to look for someone who will not know them well enough to judge them, or someone whom they consider just as worthless as themselves. This is a sick pressure because self-hatred is neurotic and because it leads to a sexual relationship with someone whom the adulterer actually despises.

c) Perfectionism

Perfectionism is an infantile pressure toward adultery. It compels people to demand the perfect situation in marriage and leaves them in a rage when they cannot find it. Every rose must blossom into exquisite beauty. Every wife must be ravishing, romantic, strong, tender, understanding, and competent; every husband must be a composite of impossible excellence: the rich provider, the imaginative lover, the tender helper, the sturdy pillar, and a thousand other conflicting perfections. Things as they are never seem right. Perfectionists always want more: they want the impossible in a world of imperfect people. So they seek the perfect situation in an enacted fantasy. Perfectionism is a sick pressure because it asks for more than any mere mortal can ever give.

d) Escapism

Escapism is a cowardly pressure toward adultery. Some people suffer from chronic "too muchness": life is always more than they can handle. It may be the children, the husband, the in-laws, the budget, or the total situation; or it may be boredom, the dullness of a life without goals, interests, or meaning. Tired of it all, the escapist simply wants to get out from under the pressures of either too much or too little in life. He or she runs. And the most promising place to run is into the arms of a promising lover. Escapism as a pressure toward adultery is not a need for love or sex, but a sickly inability to deal with responsibility.

e) Deviations

Sexual deviations make up a sad pressure toward adultery. They tempt people into adulterous situations because of shame and intolerance. A man may be ashamed of some sexual oddity or perversion he has, and a wife may be intolerant and unable to cope with her husband's quirks. The husband does not try to cure them or explain them. Instead, he runs to someone — most likely a prostitute — who is not squeamish, who has seen it all before, and who therefore will accept him with his sexual oddities.

2) *Healthy Pressures*

Pressures are not excuses. They are only factors in people's lives that sometimes shove them toward adultery. Not everyone who feels the pressure commits adultery; often adultery does not even enter the mind. But pressures do make people vulnerable should they find themselves in a situation where adultery is feasible; they do help explain why some normal people do in fact get involved in extramarital sexual relations.

a) Why Some Men Commit Adultery

(i) Boredom   After several years of marriage, the romantic dream may slowly fade and be replaced by boredom. Partners may have never tried to keep any excitement alive in their sexual relationships. They may not have grown emotionally or intellectually since the wedding day. The husband feels as though he is caught in a dull routine. Nearing middle age, he is no longer content to settle for sameness and security. Perhaps he wants to hunt, to conquer, to adventure; so he is tempted to take advantage of any available prey to his zest for excitement.

(ii) Sexual Deprivation   A husband may be married to a sexually inactive wife. Her desire may have been killed sexually by his own ineptness; in any case, she is no longer interested. She may be a passive personality; she may simply lack the spirit for interesting sexual partnership, Or illness may be a factor. Or he may simply be supercharged physically while she is undercharged. Whatever the reason, his sexual needs may be urgent and may form a pressure toward adultery.

(iii) Emotional Deprivation   A husband may be married to a chronic leaner: a woman who is a shadow, content to follow his lead. He may have grown intellectually, expanded emotionally, and be in need of a lively counterpart. But his wife has always waited on him and waited for him to bring interest into the marriage, to bring newness in their lives, and to provide sexual initiative. He deeply wants to communicate with a strong, vital, aggressive female who can bring an emotional charge into his life. The pressure need not be genital; he may have all the sexual

release he needs. But the emotional pressure can be deep: he needs someone who can aggressively feed new currents into his deeper self.

(iv) *Self-Doubt*   A man may be coupled with a wife who asks little. She provides what he wishes, is easily satisfied herself, and may even think her husband is a splendid lover. But he wonders whether he could make a truly vital woman happy, whether he could perform adequately with a powerful partner, whether he really could arouse a passionate woman to sexual ecstasy. He feels a need to prove to himself that he could really be a lover as well as a routine provider for someone whose demands are minimal.

(v) *Unequal Growth*   A man may have grown intellectually and professionally, while his wife remained stagnant. Indeed, he may have stunted his wife's growth by demanding that she only bear and rear the children at home, and cultivate no outside interests. In any case, he has developed interests his wife does not share; and he may have developed sexual inclinations his wife dares not invite him to explore. He feels as though there are still un-developed parcels in his personality waiting to be opened. He finds a woman, perhaps at his job, who brings out surprising new facets in himself that excite him. He revels in a new self that was just waiting for some woman to pry loose. His need for self-discovery in a challenging relationship is a pressure toward adultery.

b) Why Some Women Commit Adultery

(i) *Sexual Deprivation*   A wife of forty may be at her peak sexually. She feels new stirrings of sexual excitement that she had inhibited in her younger years. But her husband may have become absorbed in business, football, or crabgrass; he may be preoccupied, tired, or depressed. Thus, by the time the wife feels both stimulated physically and free emotionally, her husband has lost much of his interest; or maybe he never had any. She may be frustrated, hurt, yet fascinated and perhaps a little embarrassed by her own inner excitement. But she is vulnerable to any man who will affirm her sexuality and offer exciting promises of fulfillment.

(ii) *Need for Self-Esteem*   A woman may be wholly satisfied sexually but deeply discontented personally. This is especially true of a woman who at middle life wants finally to branch out into independent activities. She may wish to work, go back to school, or simply build a new social life. Her children are grown, and she looks back on her first fifteen or twenty years of marriage as drudgery. Now she wants to demonstrate to herself that she is, after all, a person in her own right. Her husband, used to the convenience of a dependent wife, gives her no encouragement. But other men do. Other men appreciate her as a person, not as a dutiful housekeeper. She may drift into a close relationship with one of them because of the esteem he makes her feel for herself; and thus she is vulnerable to even closer intimacy.

(iii) *Emotional Deprivation*   A woman may be married to a man who allows her to live her own life. He may be a competent sexual partner on a physical level, but he is not able to provide her with affection, tenderness, or love. She is out on a limb emotionally, desperate for affection. She discovers a man, or several men, who themselves are eager to relate to a woman who responds to affection and tenderness. Her emotional needs make her vulnerable to the tender touch of a man with feeling.

(iv) *Creeping Old Age*   Attractive women especially are pressured toward adultery when they suspect that age is cutting into their youthful attractiveness. They are anxious because they have been conditioned to prize their gift of sexual glow. Their ego gets tied to their appearance, their sense of power to turn men on sexually.

Besides, being sexually attractive, they tend also to be sexually self-conscious, sexually alive to themselves. But when middle-age brings roughness to the skin, roundness to the stomach, and sagginess to the cheeks, they become more than usually fearful. This is a price a woman pays for the gift of sexual attractiveness. It could make her vulnerable to any man who can prove to her that she is still able to attract a lover.

(v) *Independence*   The independent woman simply comes into contact with more men. For a woman who has become independent after several years of domestic confinement, this can be a heady experience. She is, in the first place, striking out on her own for the first time. Beyond the mere fact of financial or vocational independence from her husband, she feels free as a person. And at the same time she is meeting attractive men who are ready to wine her, dine her, or make love to her. Women's independence is a pressure toward adultery.

We have been looking at several pressures toward adultery that modern men and women feel. None of them is a justification for adultery. But they help explain why many married people do in fact get involved in extramarital affairs. There are, of course, many people who feel the pressures and do not leap the walls of marriage. They may be morally strong; they may only be timid; or they may lack opportunity. For whatever reason, the pressures toward adultery are not enough to push them into it. But we are concerned with the fact that many people do commit adultery. We have taken time to examine the background for adultery because it makes the moral issue the more urgent. Since people do feel pressured both by their environment and their inner experience, we must examine the moral issues as carefully as we can.

2. WHY IS ADULTERY WRONG?

We ask the question, not to throw doubt on the premise, but to clarify its moral ingredients. Adultery is condemned, sometimes, as cheating on one's partner. As a species of cheating, adultery would be wrong on that score. It would be wrong because it violates the rules by which the players agree to play the game. But cheating may be a less than adequate way — maybe a superficial way — of assessing adultery. For one reason, two people may agree to an open marriage: if they agree that their marriage contract will allow for sexual friendships outside their marriage, the only rule may be that adultery be open and above board. In this case, adultery would not be cheating on one's partner. For another reason, judging adultery as a form of cheating would be putting it on the same level with cheating on the budget. A wife could stash away part of the food budget and spend it on liquor; this is cheating. Adultery and cheating on the budget would be wrong for the same reasons, neither having anything to do with sexual intercourse or liquor.

But adultery may be a special form of cheating in a sense that touches uniquely on marriage and sex. Paul talks about the rights that married people have to sexual intercourse. This puts coitus in the unsentimental arena of justice: a wife has a *right* to sexual intercourse. "For the wife does not rule over her own body, but the husband does; likewise the husband does not rule over his own body, but the wife does" (I Cor. 7:4). So sexual intercourse is not only a matter of erotic desire but of just due. There is such an old-fashioned thing as "conjugal rights."

Sex as an obligation may grate on romantic feelings. No contemporary manual on the joys of sex is likely to capitalize on sexual intercourse as an obligation owed. But there is more to sexual life than most romantics perceive. The right to sexual intercourse is not a property right: Paul makes this clear by saying that *both* partners have rights to each other's body. "Be subject to

179

one another," he puts it in another place (Eph. 5:21). Sexual rights in marriage are the product of mutual self-giving; each partner bestows the right on the other. This happens, at the beginning, in the contract both make: a commitment to marriage is commitment to a sexual union whose beating heart is felt in sexual intercourse.

There is no marriage without sexual intercourse. Medieval scholars turned marriage into a sacrament that was climaxed at the high altar; the partners were fully married while still virgins. But Paul believes that only with sexual intercourse do two people become the "one flesh" of marriage. And it is to a life of sexual intimacy, as well as to a galaxy of other facets of life-union, that people contract themselves in the wedding ceremony.

Now, since sexual relations lie at the center of marriage, the contract to give up rights to one's body to the spouse implies giving them exclusively to the spouse. A man's wife not only has rights to his body; she has *sole* rights. And vice versa. So cheating is, after all, a basic ingredient in the morality of adultery. We must not sentimentalize everything. Marriage and sex are covered by more than erotic desire, romantic longing, and personal attachment. They are covered by the demands of justice. And cheating is a violation of the just rights of a partner.

Another case against adultery is that it tends to hurt people. And it is not difficult to find ways in which people often do get hurt. Adultery is almost always carried on secretly; it is sneaky and furtive. So it involves a kind of charade at the very center of marriage. It is thus bound to corrode all the honest and fragile personal responses of the married partners; behind everything the partners say and do with each other in intimacy lurks the charade carried on outside. Even if it happens in an open marriage, where it is done aboveboard, the spouse left behind is bound to feel rejected and unwanted — no matter how broad-minded a front he/she puts up. Moreover, not many people have the time or energy to carry on two deeply involved sexual relationships. One of them is bound to get shortchanged, and it probably will be the marriage. The third person is also likely to be robbed in the end; emotions and needs that run very deep are usually doomed to frustration. Then, of course, there is the adulterer: his/her emotions become tangled, integrity is split, roles are confused, his/her sense of being a trusted person is snarled, and he/she is plagued by a guilt that is not resolved. We surely are not mistaken in assuming that adultery almost always hurts somebody — and that it is wrong for that reason.

But if adultery is wrong only because of its painful backlash, it is wrong for the same reason that inflicting physical pain is wrong: it hurts. On this basis, if a person can handle the pain, and cause minimal hurt to others, he could choose the right time, place, and person, and go ahead. We need to ask, then, whether adultery has a special kind of wrong about it. Getting our cue from the New Testament, we would have to say that it does. It goes back to sexual intercourse as a life-uniting act that is morally fitting only within a life-union. The wrongness of adultery is knit into the inner lining of sexuality. Sexual intercourse has a mystique about it: there is something inescapably — if invisibly — special in the encounter. Most people, I suspect, still sense this, even when they do not honor it in practice. Most people who have sex outside marriage still find it necessary to invoke some powerful excuse for it — even to themselves. They need to feel like victims of some force beyond their control that is driving them to it. And they cannot place it up front within their open agenda; it must be kept on a back burner, out of sight. Some people can achieve an open marriage; few have the stomach for "open adultery." Why? Is it because we still feel a vague sense for the mystique of sexual intercourse? Even if we can convince ourselves that nobody is getting hurt, even if we are sure we are not cheating, we have a suspicion that it is inappropriate. We tend to give ourselves away; we really have not got past the feeling that adultery is an intrinsically questionable affair.

3. IS EXTRAMARITAL SEX ALWAYS WRONG?

We could play some intellectual games with this question. Moralists are good at them. They like to play the game of finding extreme cases that stretch the straight lines of simpler morality to a breaking point. They might bring up the celebrated case of the German woman who slept with a Russian prison guard so that she could become pregnant; she knew that if she were pregnant she would be released from the concentration camp so that she could join her husband and children again. So she committed adultery, and everyone involved praised her for it. However, it is not necessary for us to play games with exceptions that only underscore the rule. Instead, we want to face the more common fact that many ordinary marriages are a sexual misery. We want to ask the question in awareness that our environment pushes many people to the borderlines of adultery. We want to ask it while knowing that many married people today are feeling unique inner pressures toward extramarital sex. Do our sexual times and changing feelings about sexuality ever justify a discreet adventure into sex beyond marriage? Or does fidelity in marriage still demand *at least* keeping one's genitals at home?

We have talked about fidelity as a positive and creative dedication to the total needs of one's partner. But let us grant that we have to be realistic in our expectations. Fidelity asks very much, and few persons can give it all. Few are totally sufficient for each other. Most married people have several need levels — intellectual, spiritual, emotional, as well as sexual — all of which their spouses cannot fully meet; husbands and wives are fools if they serenely suppose they are fulfilling the whole range of their partners' needs. And only a neurotic spouse would demand that he or she alone be allowed to provide all the personal needs that human relationships satisfy. However, the issue is whether our needs provide us with an inalienable right to satisfy them.

We are defining adultery as sexual intercourse outside

182

marriage, so our interest is in sexual needs. People need more than regular sexual intercourse. They need sex with affection, with tenderness, with desire, and with passion. Some spouses can provide the mechanics of sex, but without the erotic accompaniment. A wife can be sexually starved though her husband is a coital virtuoso; a husband may be unfulfilled because his wife, passively giving him his rights, starves him for excitement. There are also wives at the peak of their sexual consciousness whose husbands, at the ripe age of forty, have traded in their sexual interests for business and hobbies.

We should mention the semitragic situations just to make the possibilities of adultery seem more fair. A husband's premature ejaculations may leave a wife limp with futility or wild with frustration. A wife's failure to reach orgasm may make sex a boring chore for her and a constant exercise in guilt for her husband. And, of course, there are the more severe dysfunctions of impotent husbands and disabled wives. We could compile a long list. But all we need is a little imagination to feel our way into the urgency of the question for some people: can extramarital sex ever be right?

One way to handle the problem is to keep extramarital sex cool. That is, if we could strip sexual intercourse of its mystique, we could perhaps find a way to approve of nonchalant affairs for the unfulfilled spouse. Keep outside sex impersonal so that one can keep his heart at home. Make it a matinee performance: martinis, lunch, and an hour at a motel — but no personal involvement, no complications, and no love. This way one might confine extramarital sex to the genitals and remain personally faithful to the spouse. But another question arises: what about the third person? Can he/she keep sex flippant in tune with the "faithful" adulterer? Or is he/she being exploited? An even more urgent question is: can sexual intercourse really be confined to the genitals? Is there something about it that will not remain flippant and casual?

183

It may even be argued that extramarital sex can be therapy for a threatened marriage. Some wives and husbands simply do not have the patience to teach their husbands and wives to be satisfying sexual partners. They have never learned to talk together about sex. So why not allow for the services of an outside expert? An affair with a competent and sympathetic person might send the inept partner back home a more confident lover. Any current manual on marriage is likely to offer successful case studies of creative adultery.

If we remember all those pressures toward adultery that men and women — each in his/her own way — feel in our time, they may help us understand why so many people today do find sexual encounters outside their marriages. But do they tell us that the old rule of minimal fidelity is really just a rule of thumb, good for most people but made to be broken by people whose sexual needs have outpaced their spouses' ability to respond? The question keeps coming back to the moral mystique of sexual intercourse. Does the New Testament know something modern people do not know? Is there still, despite what many people feel about it, an inner meaning and an irreducible mystery of life-uniting significance about it?

The Christian answer to the question of whether adultery is always wrong may sound like a loveless absolute: Yes, it is always wrong. But it could also be argued, on the basis of love alone, that it is precisely in hardship cases that adultery may do the most hurt. The sick wife, the impotent husband, the ineffective lover may be humiliated and depressed because the spouse's escapade rubs salt into wounds that hurt badly enough as it is. We must not push a person's capacity for unselfish love too far. To expect a spouse to approve of adultery may be asking her/him to commit moral and psychic suicide.

Is it possible that creative adultery is born of a demand for a completely nontragic existence? Existence without sexual frustrations is possible only in fantasies. And if we accept the tragic side of life with courage, we may be able to transcend the burdens of sexual unfulfillment. Men and women shall not live by sexual satisfaction alone. And when they discover that they can live fruitfully — if not in perfect happiness — in spite of sexual frustration, they may be on their way to a personal stature they did not dream possible.

Finally, in at least some cases, modern sexual therapy can be an alternative solution. There are many reliable sex clinics around the country (along with some bad ones), and Christian people should not feel disdainful of them any more than they need feel disdainful of any psychiatric help. With a little investigation, the reliable ones can be found. They are costly in terms of fees and time; but for some they could be the beginning of a newly found avenue to a marriage that is satisfying enough to resist the drift toward adultery.

For some people sexual fidelity is the "false god of a closed marriage." But, given the inside story of sexual relationships, it may be a courageous and loving acceptance of an imperfect marriage in an imperfect world. And that could be the foundation of a creative — though imperfect — marriage and a fulfilling — though imperfect — personal life.

4. ADULTERY OF INTENT

In spite of its concentration on genital penetration as the focal issue of adultery, Christian morality scuttles any notion that two people would be avoiding adultery merely because a gulf is fixed between their genitals. Jesus' words about adultery of the heart invalidate all cheap claims to technical fidelity. But while he cut to the heart of the matter, he also led us into a maze of moral vagaries. Further, with broadside spiritualizing of adultery comes a temptation to take on burdens of self-judgment we do not deserve. So let us take a candid look at adultery of intent.

We have already talked about needs married people have for friendships outside of marriage, including friendships with people of the opposite sex. One does not need twenty-twenty sexual vision to realize that friendships can disrupt a marriage relationship; friends can become lovers and, even if they do not, a spouse may fear that his/her partner's friend is a competitor for love. Where can we possibly draw a line? If a husband plays tennis with a neighbor's wife on Saturday mornings, he need not be a candidate for incipient infidelity. If a wife develops a friendship with a man who shares her love of chamber music, she need not be on the threshold of adultery. Only those who suspect that every friendship between a man and woman has sexual intercourse as its natural goal will label every friendship as adultery of intent.

The line between tolerable friendships and wedge-driving relationships can be recognized not by rules but by imaginative discernment. The lines must be drawn by everyone according to his own self-knowledge and his own situation. There are always three parties involved; and the decision concerning when a friendship outside the home subverts the partnership at home will depend on its effect on all three. The husband who has a woman friend will have to keep an eye clearly focused on his own emotions; he has to know when a friendship centered on shared work or hobby subtly shifts to erotic attraction for the other person. Secure in the integrity of his relationship with the other woman, the husband will also have to be sensitive to what that relationship is doing to the infinitely more important one he has with his wife. The more committed to all the dimensions of fidelity he is, the more sensitive he will be. And while he has only friendship in mind, he must be sensitive to what feelings his relationship with the third person may be setting loose in her. But life is never simple. A husband or wife may be unreasonably suspicious and carpingly jealous about every relationship the partner has that does not include him/her. What does one do about the jealous spouse? One may, out of concern for him/her, break off the outside friendship; one may also help the spouse overcome his/her fears and suspicions. In any case, all of us must watch over our relationships: every person will have to be the censor of his own inclinations and the sensitive reader of signals from the other two persons.

Jesus was not talking specifically about friendships when he warned about adultery of the heart, but he did make it plain that adultery need not involve the genitals: "But I say to you that every one who looks at a woman lustfully has already committed adultery with her in his heart" (Matt. 5:28). The soul has a sex life of its own. Jesus was not the first to make this point, it is true; rabbis had made it before him. But he was striking a blow at pop Judaic legalism. He struck, too, at the legalism of Christians who enjoy the illusion that technical chastity is all that fidelity is about. We are persons as well as bodies, and our sexual responsibility includes the mind as well as the genitals. What we do with our genitals usually involves the person; but our spirits can be sexually involved without our genitals. Legalists are not off the hook if they happen to be too timid, too hemmed in by community pressure, or simply do not have the time or energy for extramarital affairs. Fornication is possible without crossing the front steps of our inner thoughts.

But it is equally possible that we have allowed the Lord's spiritualizing of adultery to put a load of guilt on innocent consciences. So we should hazard a few observations in the hope of liberating the unduly guilty, at the risk of appearing to dull the sharp edge of Jesus' warning. There is no way of defining lust exactly; we must take Jesus seriously without pinpointing the exact edge of the precipice. To "lust after" a person must have something to do with fanning desire into a flame of specific intent. And it probably has to do with a narrow focus on another person's body.

It is foolish to identify every erotic feeling with lust. There is a sexual desire that feels like a lonely vacuum yearning to be filled, a longing for intimacy that broods unsettled in one's system. To identify this as lust is to brand every normal sexual need as adultery. Eros, the longing for personal fulfillment, must not be confused with lust, the untamed desire for another's body. Nor is every feeling of attraction toward an exciting person the spark of lust. It would be odd indeed if the Creator put attractive people in the world and forbade us to notice them. But there is a difference between the awareness of someone's sexual attractions and being dominated by a desire for that person's body. Jesus did not choose to draw the line between them. But we should know that there is a difference, so that we will be neither too quick to feel guilt nor too careless with our feelings. Attraction can become captivity; and when we have become captives of the thought, we have begun to lust. When the sense of excitement conceives a plan to use a person, when attraction turns into scheme, we have crossed beyond erotic excitement into spiritual adultery. There need be no guilt when we have a sense of excitement and tension in the presence of a sexually stimulating person; but we also need to be alert to where that excitement can lead.

What, then, of sexual fantasies? Almost everyone's imagination, at some time, produces sexually loaded fantasies. The more productive the imagination, the richer and more interesting the fantasies. We encourage the fantasies that are the stuff of literary fiction. Should we consider ourselves spiritual adulterers if the same kinds of fantasies include sexual episodes? If a teenage boy fantasizes about sexual play with a film star, is he "lusting after" the actress? If a seventy-five-year-old man fantasizes a sexual embrace with a childhood sweetheart whom he never touched in real life, is he "lusting after" her? If a woman married to a sexual clod now and then fantasizes about Richard Burton making love to her, is she lusting? Are these people actually captives of sexual desire for the person they are fantasizing about?

Fantasy life can be treacherous. If we retreat too often into that world without risks, without demands, and without disap-

188

pointments, it can become an escape from genuine encounter with real people. There is something tempting about fantasy life when real life is either dull or difficult. For people who habitually run away from reality that is less than perfect into the world where they can make everything turn out just as they wish, there is real danger. But the danger is not that of lusting so much as of unfairness to the real people who populate our real world of sexual relationships.

We must ask another down-to-earth question about adultery of intent. Is the person who gets excited by sexually stimulating photographs lusting? The answer must be that it all depends. An adolescent paging through *Playboy* magazine may be doing more than satisfying his curiosity; but he is not necessarily lusting after those faceless figures of centerfold land. A husband who is distracted, tired, depressed, and in general out of tune with his own sexuality may feel the need of a sexual stimulus that his wife, unfortunately, does not provide. If he sneaks a look at some touched-up picture of an undressed woman, he may, in fact, be merely receiving the stimulus he needs to make love to his wife. Now it may be sad that some men or women need this kind of stimulus; their spouses may have reason to put more life into their own sexual styles. But in this real world of pressures and distractions, any person who insists on being the only sexual stimulus in the world for his/her spouse is courting disillusionment. On the other hand, any spouse can become more attractive and ought to find out how. But what needs to be admitted here is that the tired husband or wife who is turned on by an erotic picture is not necessarily lusting after the person behind the image.

The moral problem of sexually stimulating literature is serious enough in our time. We have sliced physical sex from its deep roots in the person, plastered it on the billboards of the public arena, and in general deflated human sexuality by overexposure of the sexy body. But we must not translate the large public problem of pornography into a moral judgment on every person who looks at sexually stimulating pictures. On the other hand, to say that being "turned on" by erotic pictures is not necessarily lusting after a person does not mean there is no personal danger involved. Some people are sexually stupid enough to make a touched-up picture of some exhibitionist their secret standard of a satisfying sex partner. Some people are so threatened by the challenge of deep personal relations with living human beings that they escape into the make-believe world of sex idols. Erotic pictures, then, become a substitute sexual life for those who have neither the imagination for fantasy nor the spiritual ability to communicate sexually with a real person. There are sexual pitfalls in any person's traffic with pornography. However, the point is that not every second look at a picture of a nude body is qualified for condemnation as "looking at a woman to lust after her."

Nonetheless, the Christian perspective on living before God does compel us to ponder seriously and self-critically Jesus' words about lusting. God takes our inner lives seriously, not to snatch the last secret place of innocent pleasure from us, but because the inner self is at once a reservoir of moral power and a cauldron of moral turbulence. What we do within us tells God more about what we are than does the occasional lapse into external sin. A person who avoids the external act of adultery can meanwhile wallow privately in mental debauchery. He may be too timid to make an advance toward a real person, but may play bold games in the cloisters of his mind. So Jesus is saying to the legalist who lurks in everyone's soul: "Watch your heart with all diligence, for out of it are the issues of [your sexual] life."

Morality *begins* within; yet Christians should understand that "lusting" is not on the same moral level with adultery in action. Some plain words must be said on this point. Hating one's brother is a personal moral sin; but it leaves the brother breathing. Lusting is a culpable moral lapse; but lusting leaves the person "lusted after" unabused. Thinking is not the same as acting, neither in the eyes of the law nor in the eyes of God. The mind is an important moral arena, but we need not paint thoughts the same moral color as we paint actions. A child who plays "robber" in a cops-and-robbers game is not guilty of thievery. Why should a person who plays sex games in his mind be guilty of the act of adultery? Adultery of the heart is a real possibility; Jesus will not let us forget that. But humans do not have the instruments for measuring the precise difference between heart-adultery and body-adultery. Let it suffice to know that there is a difference. Adultery in action is worse, but it is better to do what we can to avoid both of them.

5. WHAT DOES ADULTERY DO TO A MARRIAGE?

We ask this question because Jesus said — in one report — that a spouse was permitted to get a divorce if his partner committed adultery. So we must ask what adultery does to a marriage. Why should it be the one reason partners can break the bond? We are not now asking what adultery does to people who are married; we are asking what effect it has on the marriage itself. Does adultery possess a strange power to dissolve a marriage bond that God himself ties? Does one act of passion unlatch holy wedlock? Does the intrusion of a third party into the sexual life of a married couple undo the unity of "one flesh" forged by personal commitment, civil contract, and the blessing of God? Or does adultery not break a marriage after all? Is it only by the decision of the partners themselves that a marriage can be broken?

I am going to be talking about adultery. This book, after all, is about sexual morality, not about marriage and divorce. But I want to ask what effect adultery has on a marriage. So I will have to ask questions about marriage and divorce. What is a marriage? What is a divorce? Is marriage an "estate" in which a person is a moral captive even after he quits the marriage by divorce? Is a divorced person — morally — a refugee from a "marital estate" that still holds him, in God's sight, forever? Or does divorce actually destroy a marriage once and for all? These questions are entangled in our main question: does adultery destroy a marriage?

Obviously, the question makes sense only if one accepts the moral authority of Jesus. If one assumes that marriage is a private affair between a man and woman, and nothing more, the question will be bewildering. But Jesus' words have set the standard for the Christian community. And some of his words about divorce have created the impression that adultery does in fact destroy a marriage. This notion has in turn had an impact on how Christian people have thought about marriage and divorce. It also works the other way around. How they thought about marriage and divorce has affected what they think about our question of what adultery does to a marriage.

The crucial words are found in the Gospel of Matthew. They were the basis for a long tradition of churchly opinion on marriage and divorce. Here Jesus said: "I say to you: whoever divorces his wife, except for unchastity, and marries another, commits adultery" (Matt. 19:9). (In another place, Matthew reports similar words, with the difference that there he does not mention re-marriage, and he says that the husband's divorce action makes his wife an adulteress — Matt. 5:32.) We will not follow the long trail of opinion about Jesus' meaning, except to draw on it here and there to indicate why our question is a very real one.

Jesus sets marriage firmly within the soil of creation's original plan for a man and a woman. Marriage, he says, was from the beginning willed by God as a splendid feature in human life. And any specific marriage is willed by God to be permanent; this is God's doing. Unless the wife commits adultery! Of course, Jesus was speaking to a society in which it would have been unthinkable for a wife to seek divorce for any reason. What could a divorcee do with her life in Israel? Had he spoken in a society of sexual equality, he would surely have included both husband and wife.

We will ignore, for the moment, the fact that Mark and Luke, in reporting Jesus' veto of divorce, make no mention of adultery as an exception. They quote the Lord only as proclaiming the permanence of marriage and allowing no grounds at all for the divorce option. For now we will linger on Matthew's adultery clause.

The first question our Lord's words pose is this: does the act of adultery itself break a marriage, or does it only provide moral grounds for the innocent partner to break it? Does the innocent partner seeking a divorce ask only for legal recognition of the fact that his/her marriage has been *destroyed?* Or is adultery a *wound* in the tissue of a deeply personal sexual partnership so serious that it gives a partner the moral right to dissolve the marriage through divorce?

In the church's dealings with marriage, there is a steady strand of opinion which says that adultery itself breaks the marriage bonds. Divorce, then, is only a legal agreement that the marriage has been broken by adultery. One does not destroy a marriage by getting a divorce; he only ratifies the rupture. When adultery happens, the marriage at that instant vanishes. But consistency is hard to come by in this matter. For several new questions intrude on the lives of people if the question is to be settled in this way. For instance:

a. Is the innocent partner *obligated* to get a divorce if the other partner commits adultery? One would think so, since if a man goes on living with his wife after her adultery destroyed the marriage, he would be committing adultery with his *former* wife. Yet the innocent party was never given more than permission to seek a divorce; indeed, he was often counselled to forgive and be reconciled to his erring spouse.

b. May the guilty party remarry? One would think so, since the marriage no longer exists; adultery has the same effect on marriage that death has. However, Jesus implies that only the innocent party is free to remarry. But why should the guilty party not also be free to marry for the same reason? Jesus does not explain. The church found arguments to prohibit the adulterer from remarrying despite the fact that the marriage was broken. It was noted that any scoundrel could escape a miserable marriage and be free to try again simply by having an adulterous affair; so it was argued that Christ's reason for allowing only the innocent partner to remarry was the protection of society against cavalier marriage-breakers. But the question of consistency still haunts us: if adultery really destroys a marriage, why should not both parties be free to remarry?

Others have contended that adultery does *not* destroy the marriage. This is not a soft attitude toward adultery; it is rather a very tough view of marriage. For it is usually coupled with the view that not even divorce dissolves a marriage. Of course, for legal purposes, a marriage no longer exists after divorce. Thus, in a superficial sense, divorced people are out of wedlock. But their position — according to this view — is something like that of an escaped prisoner: he may be roaming the streets, but in a deeper, moral sense he is still a prisoner. He still *belongs* in jail. So it is with divorced people: they may marry again and dismiss their earlier marriage from mind; but the circle is still there, and they belong inside it no matter how they feel about it. They are escapees from the "holy estate."

If the marriage is not broken by adultery, and not even by divorce, we may ask: what is it that remains intact after the people have separated? It has always been very difficult to locate a marriage in which no one lives. To deal with this, theologians have talked about marriage as if it were a kind of metaphysical entity, a reality that exists in the deep cellars of invisible being. It is like an invisible circle that continues to claim its inhabitants even after they have escaped. However, not many people have a feel for marital metaphysics.

The medieval church located the invisible marriage in sacramental grace. Grace was a bonding agent, a kind of divine epoxy that glued people together in marriage. What remained after a divorce was the invisible bond that held people together — in a moral and religious sense — even after they had gone their separate ways. Other people who think deeply about marriage see it as a "creation order." Marriage, then, is seen as an institution that God weaves within the created fabric of human life, and every individual marriage becomes an instance of the created order. What people do once they are married cannot undo the reality of the order that binds them. "Man may violate it individually by dissolving his marriage; but . . . this refusal to accept the order of creation does not cancel its existence and its continuing claim on him" (Helmut Thielicke). Neither adultery nor divorce can affect the "order" of the marriage.

In whatever way one explains *how* marriage continues after a divorce, this view clearly prohibits divorced people from getting married again. Remarriage is out of the question for a simple reason: divorced people are in deepest fact still married to each other.

Now let us fit adultery back into the problem. If adultery does not actually break a marriage, why does Jesus allow divorce when a partner commits adultery? This is the flip side of the question we asked of those who believe that adultery as such does destroy a marriage. That question was: if a marriage is in fact destroyed by adultery, why should the partners not be *obligated* to get a divorce? Now we may ask: if adultery does not destroy a marriage, and if people remain married after adultery happens, why should they be even *permitted* to get a divorce? We should now ask once more what a marriage is. We have looked — a little skeptically — at the notion of marriage as an unbreakable circle. Now let us ask whether marriage is no more than two people living voluntarily in a self-chosen, self-created, self-sustained partnership.

People who base their marriage on love's needs have little feeling for marriage as an entity that transcends their own loving wills. In romantic eyes, a marriage is a voluntary partnership created only by the decision of the two lovers involved, and it can be dissolved by their decision when love dies. When the erotic expectation of two married people is frustrated, they can decide either to plow through their conflicts into healing or call it quits when it seems hopeless. If they call it quits, the marriage is dissolved; nothing is left over but sad memories and painful loneliness. This is what divorce does. What adultery does to a romantic marriage depends wholly on the ability of the people involved to absorb it in grace and tolerance. Adultery is reason for divorce only if they decide it ought to be. But if they decide that their relationship can survive outside sexual affairs, then adultery does not destroy their marriage. The premise here is: marriage is what people make it.

We can recognize the element of truth in the romantic concept of marriage. We can also respect the truth behind the notion of marriage as an invisible circle. Somewhere between the romantic, voluntary, individualistic notion of marriage and the ontological, transpersonal notion of marriage must be the reality of marriage as God sees it. I suspect that most people who try to think of marriage within a Christian frame believe that the romantic vision is not enough even if they think the ontological vision is unrealistic. When two people get married, they do more than sign a private contract to live together, a contract they are free to cancel. The biblical phrase "one flesh" hints at a union so intimate and strong, so total in its network of shared destinies, that divorce is simply not an option. Most Christian people would agree with what Karl Barth said on the subject: "To enter on marriage is to renounce the possibility of leaving it." And the reason divorce is not an option is that marriage involves more than the wills of the people to keep it going or dissolve it.

Thus, although the personal relationship between two individuals, the loving will to be one, lies at the center of marriage, the center is buttressed by many other realities: the vows, the moral contract made by the partners, civil customs and laws, the vocation of the partnership to serve the community, the calling to serve the future generation. And, finally, there is God's will that marriage be permanent. All these together, with the personal sexual union at the center, converge to hold two people so totally and closely together that the phrase "one flesh" still speaks powerfully to us as a signal of what marriage really is. However, most of us would agree that, if worse comes to worst, if the marriage is in fact ruined by the painful failures of the partners — or by circumstances beyond their control — people *can* dissolve the marriage. We may agree that to dissolve a marriage cries out against God's loving will, that a divorce inflicts a gaping wound in the order of creation; but the "impossible possibility" remains. The permanent union whose destruction is not an option to us is in fact sometimes broken. And when it is, the marriage is dead.

We must now return to the question whether adultery does destroy a marriage. If we think of the center of marriage as the personal relationship between two partners, a center held together by several institutional straps and intended by God to be forever, we can think of adultery's effect in a realistic way. If it is true that sexual intercourse is the epicenter of the personal center of marriage, we can understand why adultery shakes the earth where marriage partners live. And if we recall that a marriage begins with a contractual vow made by two people to fulfill their sexual lives together, we can sense that adultery is a deep cut into the moral contract on which they founded their relationship. Adultery could wound the relationship at these levels beyond repair if the "innocent" partner stakes his defenses in the "one flesh" reality of his marriage. He/she may be acutely sensitive to the fact that sexual intercourse is the sign and seal of their union, and that by putting the sign and seal somewhere else, the adulterer has torn it from his marriage. But it is also possible that, in forgiveness and understanding, the "innocent" partner may not choose to interpret the adultery of the spouse as the destruction of their marriage but as a wound that can be healed by love.

Let us imagine two different marriages. First, there is John, forty years old, devoted husband. He has always believed that God wills his marriage to continue "for better or for worse" until "death do them part." But he is entranced into a flattering and exciting relationship with a beautiful woman. One wayward night he sleeps with her, although he desires a permanent relationship with her no more than he wants a permanent case of measles. Feeling guilty, he admits this fall to his wife Jane, who is devoted both to him and to the security of the nest he provides. So she forgives him. She may even relish a secret pleasure of being morally one up on her husband. And they plod onward, putting the "sin of the male species" behind them. Was their marriage broken, destroyed, or dissolved in spite of their mutual desire to build again in shared devotion? Common sense would seem to answer no. The wrong of adultery may be deeper than either John or Jane realizes; but adultery did not destroy their marriage for the simple reason that neither chose to let it.

On another end of the spectrum would be the case of Bill and Betty, who were married after a month's love affair. As it turned out, neither lived up to the other's fantasies. Bill resented Betty's cold discouragement of his sexual desires and, besides, he seethed at her domestic incompetence. Betty came to consider Bill a clod whose mental interests never got beyond Sunday afternoon football. By the end of the first year, they had lost all intimate touch with each other. After another year of bickering, hostility, and even brutality, they separated. Eros was dead; agape had never come into the scene. They separated for six months. During this time, neither Bill nor Betty was involved sexually with a third person. After the six-month separation, Betty filed for and received a divorce.

Now, if adultery alone can destroy a marriage, Bill and Betty were still married after their legal divorce. But were they? Common sense seems to answer that they were not married. We may agree that their marriage's collapse violated God's will; we may think both of them guilty for letting their marriage reach such an impasse; we may think them stupid for getting married in the first place. We might even suspect that their kind of marriage does not qualify for the certificate of "what God hath joined together." But assuming that they were really married, once they were divorced and probably long before that, their marriage had ceased to exist.

If we have the imagination to put ourselves into these situations, we will be able to say that John plowed an immoral furrow through his marriage, but he did not destroy it by spending one night with another woman. And we can say that Bill and Betty destroyed their marriage, though neither committed adultery. They destroyed it bit by bit as they failed their calling of positive fidelity. Adultery violates a creation order: this means that adultery violates the inner nature of sexual intercourse and flies in the face of God's will for it. But it neither destroys nor leaves intact some metaphysical circle called marriage, because such a circle does not exist in the first place.

To think of what adultery does to marriage apart from the possibility of re-creative grace is to play with abstractions. One cannot imagine that Jesus would approve of an "innocent" partner suing for divorce solely on the grounds that his/her partner committed adultery. For he is the Lord of the second chance, the Lord of creative compassion whose goal is always reconciliation beyond judgment. Every instance of adultery happens in a real life setting, and what it does to a marriage depends on what real people in their marriage want it to. Adultery is *always* an evil. But when it happens, compassion compels us to say to grieved parties: "Your marriage has not been broken by the fact of your spouse's adultery; but *you* can break it if you do not have the creative power to deal with your marriage in terms of what it can still be. It is up to you. What do you want?"

Adultery can wound the relationship so deeply and violate the moral contract so flagrantly that, in some instances, a genuine renewal of the marriage is not possible. It was this possibility that Jesus recognized when he provided the option of divorce in the event of adultery. But in no way is adultery able, in itself, to destroy the marriage; it depends on how weak the marriage is — and how strong the partners are. And it depends on the adultery. Jesus does not distinguish between adulterous situations, it is true. His words are not hedged with qualifications; they simply proclaim the will of God for marriage. But it is also true that not all adultery is the same. It is one thing to be "overtaken in a fault"; it is quite another thing to make a career out of adulterous adventures. One wife may trip over into a single night's madness without dreaming of destroying her marriage; another woman may flaunt a miserable marriage by spending every other weekend in someone else's bed. A man married to a woman for whom he feels no erotic desire may, in a single taste of affection's pleasures, lapse into adultery for a day; another may play the stud, grabbing the gusto of "carnal commerce" with everyone who is willing to play his game. To all alike, Jesus' words bring judgment. But they are very different in terms of what their actions do to a marriage.

In many ways, our discussion would be simpler had Matthew not gone beyond the simple absolutes of Mark and Luke. But he did not, and we have tried here to take his words at face value. Given the total gist of the gospel, and given what seems the best of compassionate common sense, we can conclude at least this: adultery by itself does not destroy a marriage. It may wound persons very deeply; it assaults the contract to which both part-ners consented at the beginning of their marriage; it flies in the face of God's will for sex and marriage; it may make a reasonably good marriage much harder to sustain. It might even trigger an avalanche of resentment and recrimination that eventually does destroy a marriage. But adultery as such does not have the power to undo a life-union.

CHAPTER TEN

Sexual Freedom in Marriage

One way to kill the joys of sexual relations in marriage is to box them into a frame of moral rules. The one thing necessary in married sex is freedom. But if it is a mistake to weigh all sex relations on a scale of right and wrong, it is disaster to measure them only by manuals of sexual performance. Free sexual life in marriage is not achieved by great sensations. Moral sexual life in marriage is not gained by finicky obedience to rules. There is a morality for sexual relations within marriage; but it is not a morality of rules, not even of the single rule — "don't commit adultery." If marriage were related to sex as a fence is to a pet dog, all we would need for a moral sex life would be to abstain from adultery. But marriage is more than a fenced enclosure for sex: it is an opportunity to let sex be a creative force woven through the partnership. So, while we will ask questions about the rights and wrongs of sexual behavior *within* the partnership, our purpose is to point the way to sexual freedom. We have discussed fidelity in general already; now we will be talking mostly about positive fidelity in the arena of physical sex. So when we use the word "sex" here, we will most often have genital sex in mind.

1. MORALS AND EXPECTATIONS

Christian morality must deal with married sex in terms of how people actually feel and think about marriage. Married people today tend to think of sex in marriage as a means of communicating love and tenderness, as a means of mutual self-fulfillment. That is, they think positively about the potential for sex to enrich their own lives. They do not think of marriage as an institutional device for keeping sex within bounds; they think of sex as a promise for making their lives happier in relationship with each other. And sexual ethics must filter into the real consciousness of married people and touch down on their actual experiences.

It is not difficult to pinpoint factors that have changed the role of physical sex in marriage.

(1) The almost universal acceptance of a variety of contraceptive devices has allowed couples to engage in sexual intercourse without thinking beyond it to the possibility of pregnancy. This means that they can concentrate on what sex does for them as persons — or what it fails to do.

(2) Erotic love is idealized as the motive for marriage. The ideal marriage is based on the erotic attraction that each person has for the other. This makes the quality of sexual relations more important to a marriage: that affects the feeling of a couple's attraction for one another, and in turn touches the sensitive nerves of their marriage itself.

(3) Our sexually saturated culture has made us more aware of our sexuality and has led people to expect and demand large benefits from sex in marriage. This has opened the door to feelings of disillusionment and frustration; married people are less willing to resign themselves to unsatisfying sex than they used to be.

(4) Women are more conscious of their own active roles in sex. They no longer see themselves having something done to them, as passive, tolerating plumbing fixtures for their husband's needs. They expect as much from sex as men do.

202

(5) People think of sex as a means of communication. Thus, far from being a mere release of tension, sex is expected to communicate the deeper feelings of personal love. This means that when sex fails to communicate love, it threatens the marriage based on love.

We do not have to decide whether the sexual expectations people bring to their marriages are good or bad. But we do have to realize that what people think they ought to expect from sex in marriage determines the kinds of moral concerns people have about sex in marriage. The situations in which moral questions arise are shaped by what people expect from sex and what people feel they ought to expect. For instance, people who have both moral sensitivity and a high expectation from sex may be caught in a conscience problem about the techniques to use in pursuit of sexual happiness. And they may have reason to wonder about the moral feelings they carry into marriage when that morality prevents them from giving the sexual responses their partners look for. The moral side of sex gets especially sensitive when one's sexual experience, far from delivering the joys our culture tells us we have a right to expect, is acutely frustrating and painful. In short, sexual morality in marriage is mostly about how we respond as persons to the possibilities and disappointments of sexual relations in a climate of inflated expectations.

2. THE BIBLE ON SEX WITHIN MARRIAGE

The Old Testament encourages a voluptuous sex life within marriage. The creation stories, for instance, validate rich erotic expectations: male and female are created for each other, and they are meant to find in each other's sexuality the promise of wholeness for themselves. Only after the Fall is there a prediction of male domination; before the Fall, male and female are partners in sexual development. The Song of Solomon is the Old Testament's clearest celebration of sensual anticipation. Its erotic excitement pulsates with sensuality: "O that you would kiss me with the kisses of your mouth! For your love is better than wine, your anointing oils are fragrant. . . . Draw me after you, let us make haste" (1:2-4). And further on: "I am sick with love. O that his left hand were under my head, and that his right hand embraced me" (2:5-6). We do not know how this raptured couple fared after ten years of marriage, but their expectations of sex were high. We can only guess that, double standards and male chauvinism notwithstanding, Old Testament couples expected a good deal of pleasure from their sexual life in marriage.

The New Testament gives very little concrete counsel on sex within marriage. Since God's grace and not sexual joy is its major theme, this is not surprising. Still, the morals of married sex could hardly stay out of the picture completely. In Paul's household talk, the question of how married people *should* relate to each other sexually does come up, and he is usually pretty austere about it. He talks of the "rights" each partner has with regard to the other (I Cor. 7:3-5): the contract of marriage gives partners "conjugal rights" to each other's bodies. He also issues some negative generalities that apply to marriage relationships: partners in marriage ought to avoid fornication and uncleanness (e.g., Eph. 5:3-4). But Paul does not provide case studies of fornication within marriage; he assumes his readers would recognize it if it happened. The command for husbands not to cause wives bitterness (Col. 3:19) could also apply to their sex lives, but he leaves us to work out the details. On the positive side, the apostle tells husbands and wives to submit to each other out of reverence for Christ (Eph. 5:20), just as he tells wives specifically to submit to their husbands (Eph. 5:22; Col. 3:18). It remains to be seen how notions like "rights" and "submission" contribute to a sexual morality for marriage at a time like ours, when the overwhelming question is how to make sex a positive, creative experience within the sensitive personal relationships of marriage.

In order to fit biblical morality to modern marriage, we will have to do more than quote texts that refer to marriage and sex. We need to see where real problems lie within modern marriage and do our best to bring the whole moral perspective of the gospel inside the sexual scene. We will have to ask how Christian love — the self-giving love of Christ shed abroad within us — ties into the sexual experience of married people today. How, for instance, does Christian love function when sex is a bore and an agony for a married couple? What does Christian morality have to tell us about adventures into novel sexual practices that our fathers probably would have only allowed into their dreams? How does Christian morality filter into a marriage where adultery is not the problem, but where good sexual relations have become an arena of conflict instead of a connecting link of love?

3. SEX WITHOUT CONCEPTION

Most married people today simply assume that conception is a secondary issue in their sexual relationships: whether or not they have children, they feel that their sexual life is not first of all for conception but for the deepening of their love. And they are right. There is no way to make the Bible endorse the idea of sex for conception only. But this does not remove sex from conception completely. Conceiving children is so intimately related to the sexual life of married people that it is morally risky to ignore the connection completely.

In making the decision to forego children couples ought to ask themselves serious questions about their motivations. Are they ruling out children so that they can have more freedom to do what they want, buy what they want, go where they want, when they want to go? Are they eliminating the conception factor from sex purely for egotistical reasons? What about the validity of sociological or ecological motives? There is no moral route to legalism here; no one is wise and informed enough to legislate for everyone else. But the morally responsible couple will ask why they set the limits they do. One very pessimistic reason given for having no children is that the world is in too sorry a state to inflict it on children. While such a view may sound noble, it is not appropriate for Christians. To surrender to so deep a pessimism is to abandon all hope, all faith in providence, all belief that God has a future for our world.

Conception is deeply interwoven into sexual relations; the fact that we have to contrive ways of avoiding conception is a hint of how deeply it is interwoven. It is doubtful whether modern couples can rid themselves of all feelings that sex is intimately tied to child-bearing. So when they decide to have no children, they ought to face their own deepest attitudes very openly. Does the decision stem from a self-doubt about their own abilities to be parents? Does it come from a bewilderment about their own role and meaning in God's world? If feelings of self-doubt are at the bottom of a childless marriage, the moral issue becomes a brand new one. It becomes a challenge to begin a new search, not simply for good sex, but for new faith in themselves.

I think, however, that we should not press the tie between conception and copulation beyond what the facts can bear. It may be true that sexual satisfaction, like human life in general, needs to be geared to a good beyond itself to sustain an enduringly deep personal partnership. But it is also true that many partners first discover the possibilities of sexual union only after their child-conceiving days are over. Freed from concern about conception, free to concentrate on their relationship and their own joys, couples often first discover that they can communicate as persons through freely loving each other in the most physical way possible.

So, the moral question of freedom from conception is: are we using our freedom responsibly? Freedom from conception may open the gates to new possibilities of personal closeness and sexual fulfillment. But sexual egotism can, in the long run, be self-defeating.

4. HOW MUCH SEX?

If sex is good once a week, it is great every day. It is as simple as that. Only legalistic hang-ups, to say nothing of antisexual hang-overs, could make frequency of sexual intercourse a moral issue. But the frequency of sex *is* a problem, if only because some people feel that it is. The moral question is not a petty matter of counting the number of times per week that a Christian couple may decently have sex. Again, the moral question is how people can and ought to deal with their relationship when the frequency of sex has become a problem *for them.*

Some fifty years ago a scenario for a couple might have gone like this: Ken, thirty, is a vital person who desires sexual intercourse with his wife very frequently. Maybe he thinks it is expected of him to show his virility; maybe he just enjoys it. But his wife cannot understand how a decent person would want sex so often. She goes along but is secretly ashamed of her husband's animal appetite. She suspects she is being used instead of loved, becomes increasingly resentful, and, at the same time, less and less satisfying as a sex partner. Meanwhile, Ken uses his wife's hostility to justify his roving eye.

Today a scenario might look like this. Peter, forty-five, is subject to chronic mild depression. He is harassed at work, angry at his wife's sloppy appearance, and is just too tired and preoccupied to get turned on to sexual relations. So he finds all sorts of good reasons to avoid sexual contact. His wife Martha has come alive to her sexuality in powerful and restless ways; she is at a sexual peak in her life. She interprets his indifference to sex as indifference to her. She is probably at least half right, for when he does have sexual intercourse with her, it is a passionless, unimaginative routine. She is resentful, agitated, and hungry. He feels half guilty and half angry.

A woman who feels that her husband demands too much of her may have either a warped view of sex or a sense of her own inadequacy as a woman. Or she may just despise her husband. The husband who shows little sexual response is probably either bored with his wife or allowing his own psychic problems to go unattended. Or he may have a hangover from his own antisexual religious training. There are a legion of other possibilities lurking behind such problems. But what are the moral obligations involved in situations like these? We could appeal to Paul's word on "conjugal rights." Marriage does entail rights, after all, even though they are of a special kind. When two people get married, each contracts to grant his/her partner the *right* to sexual intercourse. Each "has it coming"; it is his "just due." And something is wrong, morally, when married people get into moods that curtail the rights of their partners. But appealing to rights is a poor solution for a modern marriage. No wife would be satisfied if she thought her husband made love out of obligation; sex out of duty is not a promise of joy for people who expect sex to be the free expression of love.

What use, then, is morality when love fails? Can we turn romantic desire on again because we have a duty? Nothing could sound more grimly unreal to romantics than dutiful love. And yet, it is not unrealistic. The ancients believed that Eros was a demon; moderns may believe it is chemistry. But common sense tells us that much can be done for eros by willing it. Eros fails because we fail as human beings: we fail to communicate our feelings; we fail to tell our partners what annoys and angers us; we fail to tell our partners what they could do to be more attractive. And eros fails because honesty fails. Eros and will are not strangers; to restore eros, we do not have to wait for impulses from the gods of love. We can be turned on because we both *will* to discover each other's attractiveness and to make ourselves as attractive as we can. We may not ignite a fire of passion or erupt a volcano of desire, but we can at least will the way back to adequate love.

Meanwhile, the reality of agapic love has a unique potential. Agapic love could be an offensive put-down of a partner: to signal to a sexual partner that he is loved in spite of what he is — the way God loves sinners — is a sure disaster to sex. But agapic love has staying power when eros cools down. It works by sustaining a regard for the other as a person even when the flames of desire are grey ash. Agapic love is the permanent foundation on which the lines of communication can be reopened. It provides the power to do the "works of love" that can prime the pump of eros. Agape is not the direct solution to extinguished sexual desire in marriage: it is no substitute for eros. But it is a firm personal basis for a genuine effort to restore eros again.

The moral issue is never "how much sex" but whether physical sex is being integrated into a pattern of personal dedication. What happens "between the times" is more important than how many times. If both partners are dedicated to the personal life of the other and to their growth together as persons, the question of frequency will be answered in terms of concern for the needs, desires, and the conscience of the other person.

5. SEXUAL VARIATIONS

Is there a limit to sexual play in marriage? Are some forms of sexual experiments off-limits for proper couples? Is Paul hinting at "kinky sex" when he suggests that fornication is possible within marriage? Should a person think his/her partner seamy if he/she suggests oral sex? Is there a line between affectionate foreplay and sick sex? The "joys of noncoital sex" are out in the open now; maps of erogenous zones and guides to unexplored techniques are available on any bookrack. Eyeball-to-eyeball copulation is now just one of very many forms of human sexual experience. But even in marriages where no holds are barred in sexual play, there is often still a lurking suspicion that only eyeball-to-eyeball coitus is a proper sexual activity for Christian married people. Couples may throw off inhibitions in the abandon of passion; but the light of morning finds some of them wondering if they were just a bit "unnatural" the night before.

There are a number of reasons why sexual variety has come to be regarded as decent. For one thing, classy books about sexual techniques have popularized styles of lovemaking that many couples hardly dared to fantasize about before. For another, the liberation of sex from the purpose of conception alone implies that, if copulation is good without conception, then other kinds of nonproductive sex are equally good. Before, the link between sex and conception made other nonconceiving kinds of sexual acts seem unnatural; now one orifice is considered as good as another as long as it brings pleasure. The clinical discovery that the clitoral orgasm is as splendid a physical experience as the vaginal orgasm has also helped to liberate couples from the rule of traditional practices. But perhaps the specter of sensualism is lurking here also. It may be that sexual pleasure has become the false god of our time, and thus some people may have developed an insatiable appetite for ever new and exciting sexual experiences. But it is more likely that partners have simply discovered that there are many ways of sharing sexual pleasure — and that any of them can be a good way of sharing love.

But what about the biblical morality of this? We could check a concordance to see if a text might apply; but the Bible is either exceedingly particular or very general. The book of Leviticus lays down some odd rules about not having sex while one's wife is menstruating. In one place it condemns to exile a man and a woman who have sex during the woman's menstruation (Lev. 20:18), and in another place decrees only that they are "unclean" for seven days and one is not to enter the temple for that period

(Lev. 15:19-24). (Since it is hard to guess how anyone would know, one has to presume that each couple was on its honor.) The rules against bestiality and homosexuality touch on noncoital sex, but they do not apply to relations within a marriage. Other than this, the Old Testament sets few ground rules for sex within marriage; and the ones it gives are obsolete by almost any interpreter's standard.

Perhaps the key notion in the New Testament is Christian liberty. Nothing is unclean in itself, says Paul (Rom. 14:14), and this presumably includes sexual variety. But does he really include sex in his proclamation of Christian liberty? Certainly not without limits: sex with someone other than one's spouse is definitely not part of freedom from the law. And the writer of Hebrews urges Christians to "let the marriage bed be undefiled; for God will judge the immoral and adulterous" (Heb. 13:4). He most likely means only that married people are to keep their bed exclusively to themselves; but the possibility of a "defiled" bed does raise the question of kinky sex. Still, if the marriage bed is honorable for coitus, why not for a variety of other sexual play? Christian liberty sets us free from culturally invented "moral" taboos; and since there is no rule from heaven, it is likely that the only restraint is the feeling of the other person. For example, if one partner has guilt feelings about oral sex play, the Christian response of the other will be to honor them until he/she adjusts his/her feelings. On the other hand, if the partner has only aesthetic reservations, and if these are rooted in some fixed idea that sex is little more than a necessary evil anyway, he/she has an obligation to be taught, tenderly and lovingly, of the joys of sex in the freedom of Christ.

Another dimension of the morality of sexual variety is the fact that God made us body-people. Bodies are meant to play and — we can add — to be played with. There is nothing more natural than body play, and it would be strange indeed if body play were off-limits only for sexual activities. Body play can be an adventure of tenderness and an exploration into the potential of pleasure hidden in our need for love. "All things are permitted," except coercion and violation of conscience.

This leaves us in a twilight zone where everyone is simultaneously both free and responsible. Any couple exploring new territories of sexual activity ought to feel free and open for discovery of new avenues to delight. The Christian word is: "Try it. If you like it, it is morally good for you. And it may well be that in providing new delight to each other, you will be adventuring into deeper experiences of love."

6. SPIRITUAL SEX

A young person with scrupulous feelings that sex is a necessary evil may feel liberated by the thought that sex is the sacrament of love. Here is a concept that makes sex noble and beautiful — an erotic means of grace. Sex can be spiritual; this possibility appeals at once to the biblical vision of copulation as a life-uniting act and to the romantic notion of sex as personal communication. But it has its pitfalls: overspiritualizing life can be very taxing. A sacrament is "a visible sign of an invisible grace." But how do sacraments work? It seems absurd to think that sexual intercourse can create love; thus the old Catholic notion that the sacrament brings grace simply by being performed will not survive in sex. Yet it is true that one way to fan the ashes of eros is exciting sexual intercourse; it cannot create love, but it can help rescue it from slow death by boredom.

The sacramental idea of sex also has trouble with the notion that the sacrament blesses only if we think and feel piously at the crucial moment when we take it. Translate this into sex, and we get something like this: since intercourse is the sacrament of love, we ought to think and feel deep personal thoughts of love while we do it. This means that sexual intercourse ought always to be a conscious I-thou encounter. We should look far beyond the physical delights into the soul of the other person. When we feel spiritual about the other, sexual intercourse is doing its sacramental job.

This is not Christian piety but romantic fantasy. Morality has to be realistic; it is not moral to put too heavy a spiritual burden on sex. Not every occasion calls for a Hallelujah Chorus, and not every shrub can be a burning bush. There is a time for laughter and a time for tears, and there is a time for conscious personal feelings and a time for sheer physical play. Sometimes we eat and drink to the glory of God by simply relishing a good piece of beef; not every bite has to be wed to a prayer. We play best with another person when we hardly think about his sacred personhood and just share the game with him.

If sex is enjoyed within a living environment of committed love, it is a sacrament even when people have thoughts only for the physical experience. Sex should usually be a game, played for the fun of it; and just as games may be played with only the game in mind, so may sex. Inflated demands for spiritualized intercourse can be a sexual killjoy: they can make both partners uneasy with fear that the spiritual grace of sex will pass them by, leaving only its carnal delights. Then the delights can turn into shadows of fear and guilt that one or the other is falling from grace and capitulating to the flesh. Deep personal awareness of love should sometimes break through the sexual language of the night. If the hallelujah never sounds, something is wrong. But the point of sex is that it find its *setting* in a personal love — not that every act of sex be a rapturous spiritual experience. Too much spiritualization can quench passion; and when passion dies, sex is neither spiritual nor fun.

7. SEXUAL DYSFUNCTION
AND MORAL FEELINGS

Sexual dysfunction may call for clinical therapy — either physical or psychological. But it almost always gets tangled in a web of moral confusion that is extremely difficult to sort out. Failure to achieve an erection or to have an orgasm is in itself no more moral than indigestion. But people have stomachaches without giving morals a thought, while few people fail sexually without feeling some kind of guilt, or at least shame. So it is a mistake to ignore either the physical problem or the moral feeling. From an ethical point of view, it is always important to sort out real guilt from false guilt: to nourish a feeling of false guilt is as bad as to ignore the demands of real guilt. Thus the person who experiences sexual dysfunction should clear up his moral feelings as well as cure his sexual problem.

Take the problem of premature ejaculation. First of all, "premature" is a relative term. A man may not be able to control himself long enough even to begin intercourse; or he may not be able to control his responses long enough to satisfy his wife. Of course, some women may fantasize that their husbands are sexual athletes and demand too much. In any case, premature ejaculation can become a serious problem in any marriage, but more than ever in marriages with high erotic expectations. Obviously, the time between erection and ejaculation is not a moral matter — as such. But it almost always causes resentment and frustration in sexual relations; so it becomes a moral matter. Morality looms at the point of how one responds to it. Premature ejaculation is a failure to learn *how* to control. An equally simple fact is that a husband *can* easily learn control. And since his failure is bound to deprive his wife of something precious, he is morally obligated to learn how to control his responses.

The morality of premature ejaculation becomes a problem in one's feelings about it. A man who can never satisfy his wife's needs is likely to *feel* moral shame as a result of this failure — pangs of guilt that he dares not admit. He is also likely to feel shame at being something less than a virile man. He may think that he is suffering punishment for masturbation or some sexual experience before marriage. Besides, the wife's feelings are to be considered; she may feel hard resentment against a man who consistently robs her of sexual gratification. Then a husband may, in defensive reaction, become even more insensitive to his wife's desires. Marriages have broken up for less reason than that.

The moral response to premature ejaculation is, first and foremost, candor. The husband who is unwilling to talk about his problem is failing a crucial point of committed love. Talking about one's own sexual dysfunction is one of the toughest of love's challenges; but unless it is done, sexual failure can lead to marital disaster. This was less true in times when wives assumed their lot was only to take what they got. But today, when women expect as much from sex as men do, problems like premature ejaculation have become a moral challenge. Loving sensitivity will lead a husband to express his regrets at failing to fulfill his wife's needs, and it may lead him, with his wife's cooperation, to find substitute ways. But most of all, it will move him in the direction of help. Clinics in any major city can assure almost one hundred percent cure. Not to make use of one of them — after checking out its credentials — could be both stupid and immoral.

The flipside of a man's premature ejaculation is a woman's failure to achieve orgasm. Here the physical problem is more one-sided, since a man can get primitive satisfaction regardless of his wife's failure. But it will affect a sensitive (or proud) man to the extent that he feels responsible for failing to give his wife the benefit of sexual climax. Orgasmic failure as such is a *moral* problem for women only when they make it one. Moral feelings may be one of the *reasons* a woman misses out on orgasm. She may have very deep fears of sexual response because she was taught that sex is dirty. Guilt about premarital sex could also kill

215

her chances; she may suspect that she does not deserve an orgasm. She may also have other morally tinged feelings: it is possible, for example, that she is afraid of latent homosexuality and feels morally ashamed of what she suspects are homosexual feelings. Her failure may also be a way of expressing hidden hostilities toward her husband as a person. A woman may also feel a sense of shame as a *result* of her dysfunction; she lives in a culture that exalts the orgasm as an almost quasi-religious experience. Further, she may resent her husband for his failure to stimulate her to orgasm, and then feel guilty about that. Of course, these are not feelings resulting from real guilt: they are feelings of inadequacy and shame.

So what is the fitting moral response for a woman who cannot achieve orgasm? The first thing she might do is find skilled clinical help to examine both her physiological dysfunction and its possible psychological roots: her feelings toward her own sexuality, her feelings toward her husband's sexual desires, and those toward her husband in general. I think we can speak of a person's *moral* obligation to be honest with himself; and honesty may also be the best route to orgasm. The second thing a woman might do is take another look at the importance of orgasm to love. I do not mean to downgrade the fantastic climax of lovemaking, and I may sound like a smug male for even making the suggestion. But is it not possible that in touting orgasm as the be-all of every sexual experience we have compounded the problem of failure to have it? Suppose we recall that in our first lovemaking experiences penetration — not orgasm — is the crucial moment; and suppose we think of the loving act of intercourse as the finale of love. Is it then possible that, by putting orgasm on the back burner of her expectations in lovemaking, a woman might more easily achieve it? The larger orgasm looms in our sexual expectations, the more likely we are to let it become the target of our bidden hostilities and secret fears. The other side of the coin is also very real. Many women put a very high premium on orgasm because they cannot achieve it. My point is that their intense desire for it and shame at failure to have it compound their problem. In cultures where orgasm is hardly mentioned it is most easily achieved. And who knows what is cause and what is effect? In any case, sexual therapy is not difficult to obtain; and given the right moral context, most women can learn.

The important moral task is to sort out real guilt from false guilt. This is an extremely difficult task, and no one on earth can do it with precision. But if a person discovers that he feels guilty about an innocent matter, he will also discover that there is no need for guilt feelings at all. And removal of guilt feelings may be the first step toward sexual success.

We have mentioned only two of several common sexual dysfunctions. But the moral dimension is pretty much the same whether it be impotence or premature ejaculation, failure to achieve orgasm or vaginismus (painful spasmodic contractions of the vagina that result in the inability to allow penetration). Impotence and vaginismus are far more serious — and less common — problems. But the moral aspect applies similarly: both may be caused either by moral feelings or physical handicaps, and both may leave their victims with a sense of guilt. The moral challenge is to sort out real from false guilt, accept forgiveness for real guilt, and seek the expert help available to overcome the painful problem.

There is one more facet of sexual dysfunction that Christian faith may provide special power to deal with. One person's sexual dysfunction always touches on the sexual needs of the other. If marriage is built on erotic love alone, sexual failure is very critical. However, in this crisis the power of agapic love may come in to provide the staying power of personal respect and tenderness. To deal patiently, acceptingly, and lovingly with a partner who is suffering the frustrations of sexual dysfunction is a Christian possibility. This is one way to support a partner whose self-esteem has been undermined; and building self-esteem is a moral matter of the first order. More, it is a vital condition for sexual success. Grace does not demand perfection in sexual prowess any more than in personal morality, and thus experience with grace is one route to accepting failure without self-hatred. Each partner does well to remember that he may be the only effective means of grace to the other. But again, agape is not a substitute for eros. It may give patience and respect while the sexual problem is being worked on. But, at the same time, it should never be an excuse for failure to work at reversing the sexual dysfunction.

8. MASTURBATION

We have already discussed masturbation as a temporary problem of adolescence (ch. 7). But its moral side comes to special focus in marriage, where masturbation seems to be a reversion to adolescence. A married person, we may feel, should have outgrown this sneaky juvenile practice. Since it hints at an affront to the partner, masturbation can be one of the secret problems in the lives of some married people.

The case of the biblical figure Onan bears on masturbation in marriage because it involves his refusal to have sexual intercourse with a woman who would, in effect, have been his wife (Gen. 38:8ff.). He was condemned for spilling his sperm on the ground, as in masturbation: by doing that he did not meet his responsibility to provide his brother's widow with children, as he was obliged to do according to the law of levirate (Deut. 25:5). His defiance of family duty, not masturbation, was his offense. Out of this incident has grown a notion that the spilling of sperm is what is wrong about masturbation. It may have been considered wrong for this reason at one time because people believed that the male sperm contained the whole potential of a new human being; the female was considered a mere incubator for the male seed. So sperm had an almost sacred content, and to waste it was

218

to scatter a sacred trust. But we know that male sperm needs more than an incubator to produce a human embryo, and thus in itself does not hold the sacredness of human life. So we cannot locate the moral problem of masturbation in the ejaculation of sperm outside a wife's vagina.

The moral feature of masturbation, then, must lie in the aloneness of the act. Giving oneself sexual pleasure instead of working on a loving sexual relationship with the person who has a right to it — this seems to be where the problem lies. Solo sex violates what a sexual partnership is all about; besides being an embarrassing mark of immaturity, masturbation is sexual solitaire played by someone who ought to be using sex as an expression of love for the spouse. Thus masturbation may be a copout from the challenge of creating the personal closeness of partnership that is meant by intercourse, and hence may be an escape from one's partner. Sheer physical release is selfishly chosen over the personal challenges of lovemaking. If it is this, masturbation is cheap infidelity: it avoids the risk of adultery and declines the challenge of fidelity.

When masturbation is used as a regular escape from the personal challenge of partner sex, it becomes an open sesame to a fantasy life. Making love in fantasyland is very convenient: one can burst the bubble of fantasy and its people oblige by evaporating. One does not have to live with a fantasy. Fantasy people never talk back; they never complain about one's sexual incompetence; they never have personal problems they expect to be listened to; and one does not have to eat breakfast with a fantasy. Besides, the fantasy partner can be created in any form one desires: he/she can be the image of one's wildest, most childish dreams, the paragon of sexual seductiveness. And the more one enjoys sex with fantastic perfection, the more difficult it becomes to relate to an imperfect, real spouse. I am not attacking fantasy. I am only referring to the escapist syndrome that masturbation can invite through the gateway of fantasyland. Thus masturbation by married people could be an act of infidelity if it is a regular escape from real — if imperfect — relations with one's spouse. The wrongness does not lie in one's having sexual pleasure alone. It lies rather in the masturbator's denying a spouse the opportunity of a personal sexual relationship and in the flight from the vocation of partnership.

Of course, masturbation may not be this at all. We must be fair with people for whom masturbation is not an escape. For some people it provides a substitute for a relationship that no longer exists. A widow or widower, who obviously cannot replace the sexual relations that death has taken away from her/him, can at best meet some physical needs with masturbation. For this reason, masturbation may be only an empty reminder of a fullness that existed in the past. But for them masturbation may be the only means of the physical release they very much need. And if they use it, they neither desecrate a memory nor revert to immaturity. They are simply satisfying a natural need in a wholly natural and good way. We might also think of married persons whose partners are unable to have sexual relations because of illness or impotence. Further, there are couples whose sexual needs come to a boiling point at very different temperatures; for the person whose boiling point is low, masturbation, rather than being a substitute for shared love, can be a safety valve. There are also couples driven apart for a while by unresolved conflicts. For any of these, masturbation can be a temporary detour from sexual intercourse and not at all a regular escape route from personal encounter. When it is, the partner who finds a need to masturbate ought to be frank about it; and the partner who does not masturbate can accept the other's act as a stimulus to loving understanding of his/her needs.

Masturbation can also be a mutually satisfying experience when it is done together as an exploration into new forms of sharing. Far from being a subversive, self-seeking escape from a sexual relationship, it can be an exciting excursion into shared pleasure. Those who have shared in this way should not be plagued by doubt, and they may be thankful if they have been able to please one another in an act of love. This is a sensitive suggestion. Fastidious people may consider it odd, if not nasty, for Christian taste. I am not necessarily recommending masturbation, especially for people who generate guilt feelings by it. But we must be candid and fair with those for whom masturbation is a form of release they need, and with partners who find masturbation a source of mutual pleasure.

We can put it very simply: masturbation can be a fine experience of mutually pleasing sex when it is done by partners together; and it is a legitimate recourse for married persons when partnership sex is denied them. But it is wrong for a married person who uses it as a refuge from a personal relationship with his/her spouse. It can be a shared diversion; it can be a decent compensation; and it can be an escapist routine. It all depends.

9. SEXUAL RANK

Should the husband be the initiator in sexual matters? Should the wife wait passively for the male to play the leader? Is there some sort of rank built into male-female partnership, a kind of sexual hierarchy, that obligates the male to be in command? Spilling over from the biblical concept of husbandly authority, and supported by some dubious notions about the unique male character, is a feeling that the husband should be the captain and the wife an obedient follower in the bedroom. Some males may need to think of themselves as sole controllers of the sexual helm; and some females may like it that way. But there is no reason to suppose that they *should*. And I think it is important to shatter the myth of the male aggressor.

There seems to be a kind of consistency in saying that, since the wife is to be "subject" to her husband (Eph. 5:22), she should be his obedient servant in lovemaking. And Paul adds style to logic when he hints broadly that women should wear veils as a sign that they are not brazenly claiming an identity of their own (I Cor. 11:5-7); furthermore, woman was created *for man* (I Cor. 11:9). So one could jump to the conclusion that, since sexual relationships are the nub of married life, the male ought to have the privilege of deciding when, how, and whether the female will fulfill her destiny by setting his sexual table with the bounties that are his due.

But Paul does not draw a causal line from husbandly rank in general to husbandly prerogatives in the bedroom. Here each partner concedes body rights to the other because neither owns his own body anymore (I Cor. 7:3-4). When it comes to the rights and privileges of sex, it is as true as it was in spiritual affairs: "There is neither male nor female" (Gal. 3:28). Now, if both partners have equal rights to sex, neither partner has special rights or special obligations; both are "subject to one another" (Eph. 5:21). So both can be aggressors and both can acquiesce; each can take the lead and each can follow; either can be assertive and either can surrender. Or they can stimulate each other in a synchronized orchestration of their simultaneous sexual advance.

If theology puts husband and wife on equal footing in the maneuvers of love, amateur anthropologists have not always followed suit. Serious books on sexual morals still tell us about the passivity that is woven into the female anatomy and psyche. She receives, the male gives; she is the target, the male shoots the arrow; she provides the orifice, the male provides the thrust; she is weak, the male is strong. So the female naturally surrenders while the male conquers, waits for the male to make the move, and responds when the male initiates. Husbands have been known to sew a pseudo-morality out of the flimsy fabric of these misconceptions. Aggressive women, to them, are essentially emasculators of the male. If women take the lead they are unseemly seductive; if men take the lead they are properly dominant.

222

One wonders how many wives have suffered sexual poverty in silence while waiting for an indifferent husband to get a message from his dormant hormones, or how many have felt morally put down when they transgressed a husband's superior savvy of his woman's "proper place."

Actually, the anatomical differences could suggest other metaphors. Perhaps the woman was built to surround and capture, while the male was built to be surrounded and captive. Instead of thinking of male invasion we could think of male confinement. In any event, we certainly cannot build a morality of sexual leadership on the foundation of phallic power and vaginal weakness.

It may be that many women — for psychic reasons — prefer to be led into lovemaking. Perhaps many wives do want to be wooed, conquered, and made love to. They may even want this to be their lifelong rhythm. If so, I do not know whether they are reflecting the traditional direction of their culture or expressing some built-in female docility. But I am sure that every woman has the right to decide for herself when she wants to follow and when she prefers to lead. No woman is exactly the same as any other woman, no more than any male is a Xerox copy of another. So any wife has the prerogative of asking not what "women" are supposed to do but what *she* can best do in her marriage to make sex a pleasure with her particular man. Of course, even the most obedient wife knows how to stimulate her husband to make the "first" move. And when she does, who can say which of them really initiates lovemaking? Every couple has to grope its own way into a sexual relationship that honors the rights and seeks the satisfaction of both alike. The route to mutually satisfying sexual relationships is the way of trial and error, patient expectation, and exciting discovery. And the best arrangement is sexual partnership — not sexual hierarchy.

This relates back to the positive fidelity we discussed earlier. Fidelity to a spouse obligates one to seek the other's independence. And this offers a self-serving reward. A passive shadow who moves only when we move is bound to be a dull sex partner. Satisfying sexual relations need an occasional renewal of mystery: we need to discover now and then that there is more to our spouse than we had guessed. But mystery and surprise in turn need freedom: a woman must be free to make novel approaches, take new initiatives, and spring new surprises. The clod who demands passivity is going to miss out on some rewarding experiences in the long tunnel of love, to say nothing of the injury he does to his spouse.

A sexual partnership is created in equality; this is the substrate of reality. In a partnership there is no single style fixed forever in the rudiments of creation. There is no predetermined mold for one sex, as there are no set roles for individuals. It may well be that, after women's rights have been won in all the other situations of society, a wife will mostly want to "be in subjection" to her husband when he moves toward her in erotic desire. If so, it should be her own discovery.

*   *   *

Everything we have said in this chapter is rooted in the premise that the marriage of committed love is God's design for sexual freedom. It is the environment in which freedom in Christ is lived out sexually. Within the frame of committed love, sexual fulfillment is synonymous with the potential for human fulfillment in partnership; for here sex is woven into the responsibilities of personal fidelity to the sum total of the partner's needs. With the permanence of marriage as the working premise, the two people involved need not nervously calculate their sexual activities to match a complicated set of moral rules. In this sense, married love is free from morality. But the morality of sex in marriage becomes the morality of personal response to the possibilities that creative fidelity offers for sexual happiness. Here, in this settled union, two people can adventure into sexual growth, work through sexual pain and frustration, love through the rise and fall of erotic desire, work out the stresses and ambiguities of a sexually equal partnership, and laugh at themselves for taking themselves with a seriousness that grace makes obsolete.

Second Thoughts

Everybody has second thoughts sometimes. We all need a chance to reach back and retract something we once said, maybe yesterday, maybe years ago. I'm thankful that the people at Eerdmans have asked me to read *Sex for Christians* again to see if there are some things in it that I'd want to fix. Maybe take some things back, say some things more clearly, perhaps add a few words. But as I read the book again, after almost two decades, I am mildly pleased at how most of it still seems right to me.

Still, times have changed, and I have changed some with them. Sexual morality in our secular culture has broken down miserably since I wrote the book, and its crumbling has crippled our common life. So there are reasons after all to add an afterthought or two to what I wrote about the morals of sex a couple of decades past.

Were I writing the book today, I would want, for one thing, to explain at the outset how biblical teaching about sex can still be a guide to how we should feel about our sexuality and how we should express it in our lives. The Bible is my primary authority for interpreting human sexuality. But the Bible is not the only voice I listen to. I listen to reality around me and in me as well. I need to listen to reality as well as to the Bible or I could never know how the teachings of the Bible apply to real life.

The Bible, after all, is an ancient collection of books written by scores of human writers living centuries apart from one another, in languages few of us can read today. It mainly tells the story of what God has done in the world to save it from itself. It is not a book about sex. It is certainly not a manual for sexual conduct. It is a storybook. How that ancient storybook can guide us toward the right ways to live sexually in the modern world is not always easy to say.

It is important to remember that the Bible has more than one way of teaching us how to live our lives in our time and place. Let me mention a few.

The most important way the Bible teaches is by telling us a story.

First and foremost, of course, it tells the Epic story — I mean the story of God's ways with the human family. It sets the stage for the story by telling us about creation. The plot unfolds with the story of how the first couple went wrong. And then the story really begins. It reaches its climax when God became a human being and died on the cross. It comes to a happy ending when Christ comes back to make the world right again. And all God's children live happily with him forever and ever.

We are all writing our own stories, as God wrote and is writing his. We write a large chunk of our stories as we decide what to do with our sexuality. The stories we are writing must somehow fit into God's story. So the deepest moral question we can ask ourselves is this: Am I writing my story in such a way that it fits into and contributes to God's story?

So when we wonder how creatures like us, stuck as we are with our persistent sexual urges, should live, we can always ask ourselves how what we are doing today fits into our life story and how it fits into God's story. But this is all quite free-wheeling. We do not get specific direction for sexuality from the big story. For specifics, we need some rules.

The Bible has rules, lots of them, an enormous variety of them, issued to very different people in vastly different times and circumstances. Some of these rules give us what we call moral absolutes. These are rules meant to be obeyed by all people always, no matter where and when they live. The laws of love and justice are absolutes. The commandment against adultery is another.

But many Bible rules are more like rules of strategy — rules that pointed people to the best ways for them to live as children of God in their particular circumstances and at that particular time. Paul's rule that women should wear veils when they prayed (I Cor. 11:5) and that slaves should not seek their freedom (I Timothy 6:1-2) were rules of strategy. So were Moses' rules about the extreme punishments for men who practiced sex with other men (Lev. 20:13) and the extreme measures that should be taken against married couples who had sex while the wife was menstruating (Lev. 20:18).

The rules of strategy were not meant for everybody all of the time. They were rules that may have been wise and right for a given situation. But they are not rules we live by now.

The Bible, then, tells us what to do by telling us stories and giving us rules. But neither the stories nor the rules are sufficient for us when it comes down to many of the concrete decisions we have to make in our time and place. The stories are not specific enough. And some of the rules do not apply to us.

There is, however, another way. St. Paul calls it the way of *discernment*. Here is one verse that tells us how important St. Paul thought discernment is for anyone who wants to know the will of God.

> I pray that your love may abound more and more, with knowledge and discernment, so that you may approve what is excellent. . . ." (Phil. 1:9)

To let the point of this verse sink in, we need to notice four things that it tells us.

First, we need *knowledge*. We need the facts about reality. If we do not know the facts, we will surely bungle when we try to apply the Bible's rules to real life. And, of course, we get the facts by looking at reality.

Second, we need *discernment* — which takes us a step deeper into reality. Discernment is the ability to see what is *really* going on beneath the surface of the facts. To see the difference between things. To see the connections between things. To see what is more important and what is less important. Discernment is a person's sense for the reality within reality.

Third, we need *love*. Love opens our eyes to real people. Love helps us to see beyond our self-interests into the needs and the rights of other folks. Love opens our ears to the sobs beneath the yells. It opens our eyes to the pain beneath the anger. Love helps us discern the deeper realities of real people as they struggle on their life journeys.

Fourth, the point of it all is to recognize and follow *the more excellent way to live*. Sexual morality is not simply about what is right. It is about what is good, and about what is even better than good. It is about what is excellent. For doing what is right, we need rules. For doing what is excellent, we also need to discern what is really going on around us.

Of course, nobody has perfect discernment. If anyone tells us that she knows what is right because she has 20/20 discernment, we should always get a second opinion. This is why we need to be members of a discerning community (past and present) where people share how they see things. This is what I shall be doing here; I am going to share with you how I see things. And you can match your discernment of things against mine.

We thus have two major sources of authority: the authority of God's Word and the authority of reality as we discern it. Without the Bible, we have no final reference point. Without discernment, we do not know how to understand what is going on in human sexuality or how to apply the Bible's teachings to it. We need both the guidance of the ancient Bible and the discernment of today's reality.

In this book I have focused on the sorts of people we *are* and what we *do*. We *are* sexual persons. We *do* sexual things. The two questions that match these two foci are these: (1) How should we feel about our sexuality; and (2) what sorts of things are good to do with it?

I will begin with some comments on how Christians may feel about what they are, about their sexuality.

When I wrote *Sex for Christians* we were just beginning to realize that we were living in a sexual revolution. Many of us liked much of what that revolution was about. We were glad to be reminded that God liked sex and that he wanted us to like our sexuality. So we chucked our shame of sex and celebrated being sexual. Sex was for Christians and Christians could be for sex.

I have sobered some since then. Earlier I spoke critically, even a bit meanly, of Augustine's negative feelings about passion. Today I have more respect for Augustine's reservations, and I apologize to the saint. I still believe that sex is one of God's better ideas. But I wonder whether it isn't proving a hungry tiger too tricky for fallen people like us to tame.

Are we really better off — on balance — with these wild-eyed sexual ogres dancing inside of us? They drive us crazy. They destroy marriages. They embarrass royal families. They drive ministers of the gospel into shame. They push young children to conceive children they cannot care for. They make fools out of the wise and sinners out of saints. Did God really mean to stick us with this insatiable, this crazy-making hunger?

If I were writing today, I think I would mute my celebration of sex a little. I would not want to call off the party, but I should be more wary of the inevitable hangover. Sex is God's good gift; it is also one of the most powerful urges in the human arsenal. It is not at all clear that we are strong enough, smart enough, and good enough to know how to use it well. We all need help.

Clearly AIDS is the deepest shadow that has fallen over sexual morality since I wrote *Sex for Christians*. We knew nothing about AIDS at the time I wrote. Thousands upon thousands of people were already carrying the AIDS virus inside of them. But we did not know it until later.

Does AIDS change the morals of sex?

Before AIDS, the secular standard for good sex was consensuality. That is, good sex was any sex to which both parties freely consented. Now we have a an additional standard. Good sex is safe sex. What this comes to is that any sex that does not put other people at risk to the AIDS virus is good sex. In broad stroke, then, good sex is safe sex that both partners agree to engage in.

An American basketball superstar confided to the world not long ago that he was infected with the AIDS virus. He was given a national ovation for the courage he displayed by going public. This man had been having sex with a large number of women, and God only knows how many he may have infected with the dread virus. The media considered it horrid taste for anyone to mention this moral shadow side of the story. Now our superstar is a champion of wear-a-condom sex. But the safe sex he now preaches does not come within ten thousand miles of the biblical ideal of moral sex.

The point is that our culture tells our children that any sex that is AIDS-safe and is not forced on one's partner is good sex. The children of our culture are listening. And acting. But as they grab for all the voluntary sex they can get, they do not have time to be concerned about safety. Let alone for the welfare of the children they conceive. Or the right or wrong of what they are doing.

Most Christians, I suppose, do not think that safe sex is enough to satisfy the biblical ideal. Certainly, sex should be safe. And it should be mutually agreeable. But these are minimal standards. According to the Bible, sex is morally good, and safest too, when it is an expression of love with one's marriage partner. What we need to know is that safe sex is not necessarily good sex, but that morally right sex is safest sex.

What should be the strategy of the Christian community in view of the very present dangers that promiscuous sex poses to human life?

There are three options.

One option is to support the cause of safe sex. The fact is that a great many young and not-so-young people do not live by Christian sexual standards. By supporting safe sex we might be saving some of their lives. This may mean that we would support teaching youngsters at school about the risk of AIDS. It might also include making condoms available to everyone who asks for them.

Another option is to preach the one right and the one safe way to practice sex: keep sex within marriage. We could summon our culture back to God's and nature's way. No compromise! No encouraging people to have safe immoral sex! Make it clear that it is either morally right sex or no sex.

Still another option is to do both. Christians could teach God's way as the better way. But out of compassion for those who are not listening to us, we could try to protect them from the consequences of their own folly by urging them to use condoms.

Which is the right way, and how do we know it when we see it?

It seems to me that discernment of our situation compels us to try to reduce the risk that young people are taking with sex. And one way to do it is to help them be as safe as possible even if they choose not to be as moral as possible. And this may mean that, in an imperfect world where AIDS is a horribly threatening presence, we may have to support a public policy that falls short of our personal moral convictions. In short, as I discern things, teachers should do all they can to promote safe sex as well as moral sex. Other people believe that we will undermine our teaching of moral sex if we stress safe sex. I think that, in the circumstances, we shall have to take the risk.

But AIDS is not the only tragedy that can follow careless sex. Babies are part of the tragedy too. Fatherless babies. Very many babies. In the city of Los Angeles alone, in one year, 24,000 babies were born to unmarried child-mothers. These are children whose chances of a productive, prosperous, and happy life are frighteningly poor. They too are the tragic victims of a sexual morality that tells young people that any sex is good provided it is safe and freely consented to.

What is really going on inside the sexually untamed young people of our time? God only knows the whole story. But I discern a desperate need for personal intimacy to fill the void left in the wilderness of broken families. They hunger for a closeness they do not get at home. They long to love and they hunger for love. Ask a child-mother why she loads herself with the burden of a child: time and time again, social workers tell us, a thirteen- or fourteen-year-old girl is likely to say: "I did it because I wanted somebody to love." Of course, she does not have a clue what it takes to love a baby. But she knew what she wanted and she knew how to get it.

This may be a good time to say something about the chapter in *Sex for Christians* about what we used to call petting — touching each other in sensitive places without intending to have intercourse. To some readers I seemed to be offering young people a license for illicit sex. Others tell me that the whole question is beside the point today. The worry about petting has to do with the risk of sliding down the slope of sensuous touching into illicit intercourse. And the reason they say that petting is no longer of moral consequence is that for today's young people sexual intercourse carries no more moral meaning than brushing our teeth. If intercourse has no moral meaning, it is clear that petting has none.

I think *all* sexual relationships are morally important, but I also think that not all sexual relationships are covered by moral rules. Which led me to say in *Sex for Christians* that the moral criterion for petting is responsibility. Responsibility is the ability to respond. When we make a response to something, we are giving our answer to the question that the situation asks us. In petting, one person is, in effect, asking the other what he or she intends to do, or wants to do, or ought to do. And the responsible person is able to give a genuinely human, caring, and careful moral answer.

To be responsible, what we need is discernment. We need a sense for what is really going on with us once we get into touching each other's bodies. We need to sense what is going on so that we can hear the question the other person is asking. We need to discern what is really going on with us if we are going to help each other to be more responsible for what each of us is doing.

I still believe that the answer to the question of how much petting is morally good has to be given in terms of acting responsibly. Responsibility is the key simply because there are no clear moral rules that tell us what parts of another person's body we may touch and fondle at different stages of our relationship.

Today, however, I would add that when there are no clear moral rules, we need to make our own rules. Rules of strategy. Not moral rules for everyone, but rules that tell us how far to go and when to stop. We can make our own rules of strategy so that we will know in advance what we will do before we get blown away by the whirlwinds of passion.

A sports reporter once asked Dave Dravecky, a great relief pitcher for the San Francisco Giants, what he thought about when he was sent out to pitch at a critical moment with the game on the line. Dravecky said: "If I waited to do my thinking until I got on the pitching mound, I would lose every game. I have to plan ahead of time so I know in advance what I will do when I face the challenge." Good advice for people trying to do the right thing in the game of sex: plan your strategy ahead of time.

Making rules is good strategy. The rules we make are not on a par with the Bible's Thou Shalt's and Thou Shalt Not's. But they can be helpful, especially when feelings whisper to us that we are prisoners of a passion too strong and emotions too beautiful to deny.

This brings me to a popular sex strategy called cohabitation — living together before, or instead of, getting married. People may do it to learn whether they want to marry the person they live with. Some do it to cope with loneliness. Others simply are pooling rent money. In Sweden most married people have lived together before their wedding. In the U.S. these days almost half of newlyweds have lived together at least for a while. Whatever their reasons, a lot more people live and sleep together without having a wedding than they did when *Sex for Christians* was written.

Are people better off for living together? If we are asking whether they have a better chance at a lasting marriage, the statistical answer is No. In fact, research in both the United States and Sweden has shown that people who live together before they get married are more likely to break up than people who do not live together until they are married. What is more, they are likely to repeat the process. As sociologist Andrew Cherlin observed in his 1992 study *Marriage, Divorce, Remarriage,* the pattern is this: Cohabitation — Marriage — Divorce — More   Cohabitation — Remarriage — Divorce.

But, apart from the statistics, what of the ethics of living together? Are weddings the only qualification for legitimate sexual intercourse? I don't think so. Commitment is the moral factor. People can be — and millions have been — committed to each other in marriage without having what we would recognize as a wedding. And people can have a wedding without being committed. But nobody can have a decent chance for a lasting marriage without commitment.

Many people today do not even know what a commitment

is. They think they are making a commitment when they are only making a deal. Or a contract. But a contract is not a commitment. We draw up contracts so that each of us will know what we have coming and what is expected of us. And the contract assumes that if you don't get what you contract for, you may call the deal off.

A commitment is a "no-matter-what" kind of promise. You don't make a commitment when you say, "I'll stick around so long as I am getting the satisfaction my contract calls for." In a commitment one says, "I'll be with you even when I am not getting everything I want." Which is the way God committed himself to us.

Of course, commitment-makers do not have to be fools. They know that it is extremely important to make commitments to the right persons. They know that sometimes a commitment should not have been made. And they know that sometimes a commitment cannot be kept. To believe in commitment does not require us to be unbending absolutists. The point is that committed people do not enter the relationship with qualifications. They begin with the total intention to be there and stay there for each other no matter what.

Uncommitted people tend to split. Half of all marriages in America end in divorce. And most divorced people have produced at least one child before they leave each other. Fewer than half of all children born today will live out their childhood with both a father and a mother. And a large percentage of children whose parents break up once will go through another family collapse before they grow up. So the ethics of sex in an uncommitted culture has become the ethics of how to honor a child's right to live in a stable family.

A growing body of social research shows that children of single parents do not fare as well as children of two parents. Children of single parents are six times as likely to be and stay poor. Twenty-two percent of the children of one-parent families will experience poverty for at least seven years. The National Center for Health Statistics reported in 1988 that children of single parents are two to three times as likely to have emotional and behavioral problems. They are also more likely to drop out of school, get pregnant when they are adolescent, and be in trouble with the law. Divorce hurts children. Having children out of wedlock hurts children.

I may sound unkind to single mothers. I do not mean to be. Single parents can be wonderfully strong and generous. My mother was a single parent who brought up five rambunctious kids back when there was no welfare money for mothers of dependent children. I need no lesson in the courage that single mothers have and the help that they need. But I am not talking about the courage single mothers need to bear their burden. I am talking about the uncommitted sex that loads the burden on them.

The rule that ties sexual intercourse to committed love is embedded in the law of humanity. Abuse sex and you abuse your humanity. The society that ignores the law of sexual morality ends up wounding its own children.

And now it is time for us to explore the most emotional area in the territory. I mean the morality of homosexuality.

Homosexuality is a mystery. But then heterosexuality is a mystery too. So why should we expect homosexuality to be simple?

Another mystery is why heterosexual people get as fevered as they do about homosexuality. It is certainly appropriate for heterosexuals to size up homosexual behavior from a moral point of view. But why the furious fuss that many heterosexuals create when they aim their moral guns on gays and lesbians?

What danger to straight people lurks within homosexuality? Do homosexual people threaten the family? How? Homosexual people grieve that they cannot establish a family themselves. Will they abuse our children? Heterosexual people abuse children far more often than homosexual people do. Do homosexuals as a class threaten to invade our homes, steal our goods, rape our daughters, pollute our air, or blaspheme our God? I do not think so. Homosexual people are as law-abiding and Christ-loving as any other class.

In a world of violence on the streets, a world of starving children, cruel tyrannies, natural disasters, and human greed is homosexuality the issue that we should get most steamed up about?

I think I was essentially right in what I said in *Sex for Christians* about homosexuality. I still believe that the Creator intended the human family to flourish through heterosexual love. I still believe that homosexuality is a burden that homosexual people are called to bear, and bear as morally as possible, even though they never chose to bear it. I still believe that God prefers homosexual people to live in committed and faithful monogamous relationships with each other when they cannot change their condition and do not have the gift to be celibate. My mind has not changed in any basic way since I set these opinions to paper nearly two decades ago.

I would like nonetheless to add a little more about what I discern in homosexuality and how I relate what I discern to what I read in the Bible. I will begin by pointing to some important things that the Bible does *not* tell us about homosexuality and homosexual people. Remember that the Bible does not contain a moral treatise on human sexuality. And what it does not say can be as important as what it says.

1. *The Bible does not tell us anything about a condition called homosexuality.*

The Bible observes that certain males were making love with other males. And females were making love with females. It tells us God did not approve of what they were doing. Probably the biblical writers assumed that these people were heterosexual people who were acting contrary to their own normal inclinations. The writers do not appear to have known anything about *a human condition called homosexuality*. That is, they do not even consider the possibility that a male may be disposed toward love for other males, disposed from before birth, disposed in his very being.

2. The Bible does not tell us how people get to be homosexual people.

Scientific research offers evidence that some people are genetically disposed toward homosexuality. It is bred in their bones. They are victims of a genetic accident. Maybe the errant chromosome is set loose by a slight shaking of their biological building blocks. Maybe their sexual orientation is settled for them by a quirk in the chemistry or the electronics of their brains. In any case, there is evidence that people's sexual orientation is set before they were born, the way it is decided that they will be a boy or girl. Not everyone accepts the evidence for a genetic cause. Many still hold that early childhood experience pushes some people into homosexuality. Genetics may make some children more susceptible to the influences of their environment. But, they argue, it is the environment that does the damage. Who can say for sure?

Whatever the link between genes and environment, homosexual people are stuck with what they were stuck with. They did not choose to be what they are. They only discovered what they had always been. And, for most of them, their discovery brought them pain and shame.

Thus, it seems clear that gays and lesbians are no more responsible for being homosexual than I am for being heterosexual. And therefore God does not judge them for being homosexual any more than he rewards me for being heterosexual.

3. *The Bible does not tell us whether homosexuality is curable.*

If people decided on their own account to love members of their own gender, the way a person decides to smoke cigarettes, they could be cured the way a smoker can be cured of smoking. But if a person's genetic code predestines him to be gay, his cure is going to come very hard, if at all.

With God all things are possible, but not everything is likely. God does not do everything it is possible for him to do. I know gay people who have prayed for change with all their hearts' passion. They have linked up with charismatic healers. They have spent thousands on therapy. But though they changed in many other healthy ways, they did not move an inch away from their homosexual base. When they prayed, they received the same answer Paul got when he prayed for God to remove his thorn: "My grace will be enough for you."

4. *The Bible does not tell us about the sorts of person homosexual people are likely to be.*

The Bible (Rom. 1:26-27) tells us that God at one time permitted heterosexual people to lapse into homosexual behavior. But it does not speak about the sorts of people that homosexual people are.

The Bible does not tell us about the character of homosexual people as a special class, any more than it tells me about the character of my fellow Dutchmen. It tells us only that we all have fallen short on character and that Christ died for the likes of us all. What I know about homosexual people is what I discern as their friend and neighbor and, sometimes, Christian brother.

What one may discern from knowing them is that homosexual people are as moral and spiritual as heterosexual people are. They are as likely to be honest and courageous and loving as any other class of people is. They are as likely to love God and seek God's will and mercy as any heterosexual is.

5. The Bible tells us that homosexual behavior is unnatural, but does not explain why it is unnatural.

The word "unnatural" suggests something abnormal, ugly, and abhorrent. To some of us these words are the right words to describe homosexuality. But let us not forget that St. Paul also says that it is against nature for a man to wear long hair (I Cor. 11:14) and for women to curl their hair or pray without a veil (I Cor. 11:6, 13).

What makes homosexuality unnatural? Traditional moral teaching held that homosexuality was unnatural because it could not produce children. Homosexuality goes nowhere; it always stops short of doing what sex is supposed to do. Sex, practiced as nature intended it to be practiced, produces offspring. Sex is meant to keep families going from one generation to the next. Sex that cannot produce children goes against the creative stream of nature.

Not many people accept the traditional teaching about the purpose of sex anymore. Most people, Christians included, believe that sex is for achieving intimate, personal, loving union with another person. Having children is no longer considered the fundamental reason God created us sexual. The modern Christian, therefore, has given up the traditional reason for believing that homosexual activity is unnatural. The belief that sex is mostly for love and incidentally for children removes the deepest reason for claiming that homosexuality is against nature.

6. The Bible does not tell us about the personal quality of homosexual relationships.

St. Paul tells us in the first chapter of Romans that God abandoned certain people to their lusts as punishment for their ingratitude. Some people conclude from this that what passes as homosexual love is a false front for a cesspool of lust.

But anyone who knows homosexual people knows that they can love each other as spiritually and nobly as heterosexual people can love each other. Listen to the loving longing of one celibate gay Christian man for a person he loves: "My mind, my affection fastens on . . . the loveliness of his character and the beauty of his form. . . . My love is clean and noble. Why may I not live with him as my other?" Does this man's longing smack of brute lust?

These, then, are some things the Bible does *not* tell us about homosexuality. What, then, should we think about the morality of homosexual behavior in the light of what the Bible does say? And in the light of what we can discern in the lives of real people? Here is a summary of what I think:

I think that homosexual people are not responsible for their sexual orientation toward loving people of their own gender.

I think that, as a class, homosexual people are as moral, as spiritual, as decent and good, as creative, and as much in need of the grace of God as heterosexual people are.

I think that homosexuality is not the sexual orientation that God intended in creation. It is a genetic lapse. It is nature gone awry. There is tragedy in it. And homosexual people are called to live as morally within their tragedy as the rest of us are called to live within whatever tragedy may be ours.

I think that homosexual people merit the same rights and bear the same responsibilities within society that anyone else does.

I think that, if celibacy is not possible, it is better for homosexual people to live together in committed monogamous relationships of love than not. Homosexual partnerships that are committed offer the best moral option available.

These are some things I have come to believe after studying the Holy Scripture, after reflecting on Christian tradition, and after trying to enrich my knowledge and discernment with the insight of love. I may be wrong. I may not be seeing reality as clearly as I think I am. I am willing to learn from those who are willing to share their discernment with me. But this is what I believe.

Enough then of my second thoughts about *Sex for Christians*. I have become stricter in some things and more flexible in others. But in the important matters, I have merely tried to say some things more clearly than I said them before. To paint them in different tones. For the most part, I find myself reaffirming my belief that the sexual ethic of the Judeo-Christian tradition is the best bet for humane and happy sex.

Sierra Madre, 1994   Lewis B. Smedes